Medication Use:

A SYSTEMS APPROACH TO REDUCING ERRORS

Edited by Diane DeMichele Cousins, RPh

JOINT COMMISSION

Joint Commission Mission

The mission of the Joint Commission on Accreditation of Healthcare Organizations is to improve the quality of care provided to the public through the provision of health care accreditation and related services that support performance improvement in health care organizations.

Joint Commission educational programs and publications support, but are separate from, the accreditation activities of the Joint Commission. Attendees at Joint Commission educational programs and purchasers of Joint Commission publications receive no special consideration or treatment in, or confidential information about, the accreditation process.

ISBN: 0-86688-522-6

Library of Congress Catalog Number: 98-86403

For more information about the Joint Commission, please visit our Web site at http://www.jcaho.org

CONTRIBUTORS

P Mardi Atkins, RN, MPA
Manager, Nursing Quality Management
The Cleveland Clinic Foundation
Cleveland, Ohio

Louis D Barone
Department of Pharmacy
The Cleveland Clinic Foundation
Cleveland, Ohio

David W Bates, MD, MSc
Assistant Professor of Medicine,
Harvard Medical School
Medical Director, Brigham and Woman's
Physician Hospital Organization
Boston, Massachusetts

Diane DeMichele Cousins, RPh
Vice President, Practitioner Reporting
Programs
United States Pharmacopeia
Rockville, Maryland

Maja Gift, RPh
Interim Director of Pharmacy
Pharmacotherapy Specialist,
Quality Improvement/Outcomes
Tampa General Healthcare
Tampa, Florida

Linda S Hanold, MHSA
Deputy Director, Department of Research
and Evaluation
Joint Commission on Accreditation of
Healthcare Organizations
Oakbrook Terrace, Illinois

Deborah M Nadzam, PhD, RN
Vice President, Performance Measurement
Joint Commission on Accreditation of
Healthcare Organizations
Oakbrook Terrace, Illinois

Annette Rubino, MBA, CPhT
Performance Measurement Analyst
Joint Commission on Accreditation of
Healthcare Organizations
Oakbrook Terrace, Illinois

Philip J Schneider, RPh, MS
Director, Latiolais Leadership Program
Clinical Professor,
College of Pharmacy
The Ohio State University
Columbus, Ohio

Bruce E Vinson, PharmD
Administrative Director for
Pharmacy Services
Baptist Memorial Hospital
Memphis, Tennessee

CONTENTS

FOREWORD

Five years ago, few would have thought of publishing a book titled *Medication Use: A Systems Approach to Reducing Errors*. While medication errors have always been with us and have long been recognized as a major cause of patient injury, their control has eluded our best efforts.

Past attempts to reduce medication errors have focused on education, the development of rules and procedures for safe handling, and training of personnel in consistent application of those rules and procedures. It is now apparent that while education, training, and the enforcement of rules comprise the essential foundation of safe medication practices, they are not enough. Health care is beginning to recognize what the aviation industry learned decades ago: even the best trained and most highly motivated people inevitably make errors. However, errors can be prevented by designing our work systems so that errors are difficult to make. Properly designed systems also make it easy to recognize and intercept any errors that "slip through" before they result in injury to patients. This is the essence of the systems approach to error reduction: focus on the processes, not on the people.

The cause is urgent. The toll of injuries due to medication errors is staggering. Nearly 30 years ago, Barker studied the medication administration process and found errors in 20% or more of doses administered. While most of these errors were harmless, some resulted in patient injuries. Recent studies have focused on the injuries, called *adverse drug events,* and found that as many as 10% of patients admitted to tertiary hospitals suffer an injury related to the use of a medication. One-third to one-half of those are due to errors and thus are preventable. If the adverse drug event rate in *all* hospitals averages "only" half of this (5%), more than 1.6 million hospitalized patients may be injured by complications of drug use each year. The number of injuries in nonhospitalized patients may be even higher. The cost of these injuries has been estimated at $77 billion per year.

Fortunately, health care is waking up. Publicity surrounding a series of tragic and egregious mistakes has led to increasing public concern and calls for hospitals to take responsibility for patient safety. *Medication Use* is a response to that need. Not only will the reader find a comprehensive discussion of the nature and extent of medication errors, attention is also given to the problems of measuring those errors and the effects of remedial efforts. The application of systems changes to prevent errors is described, together with examples of systems changes that have been demonstrated to be effective and a workbook section providing step-by-step instruction on how to assess systems failures and develop changes. There is much good information here. I hope it will be widely read.

Lucian L Leape, MD
Adjunct Professor of Health Policy
Harvard School of Public Health
Boston, Massachusetts

INTRODUCTION

The information presented in this book reflects the work of some of the most prominent medication errors experts in practice, reporting, research, and standards. Their collected observations and methods provide a type of resource never before published or documented in a single place. If you are not already convinced that a systems approach is the way to reduce medication errors, *Medication Use: A Systems Approach to Reducing Errors* will convince you. If you have wanted to institute systems analysis and did not know how to begin to document or measure variations in the medication use process, the guidance is provided here. If you thought keeping medication errors "under wraps" in your facility was for the greater good, you will find evidence to the contrary in the experiences of other organizations, their approaches to solutions, and their suggestions for avoiding future errors.

The first four chapters of this book present the information you need to understand the medication use system, its processes, and how errors occur. They provide suggested methods for collecting data, identifying medication errors and opportunities for improvement, monitoring your system, and integrating a systems approach throughout. Chapter 1 defines the medication use system as a combination of interdependent processes spanning the continuum of care from drug selection and prescribing through use and system monitoring. Deborah Nadzam presents the "Six Rights," along with 16 processes fundamental to building an effective medication use system. The multidisciplinary responsibilities of health professionals in ensuring the "right result" are described, and the vital role of the patient as a partner in processes is addressed. The chapter ends with several useful strategies you can implement to strengthen your own medication use system.

In Chapter 2, Philip Schneider and Maja Gift point out that improving processes requires commitment (in particular by management) to identify, measure, and analyze errors, as well as an infrastructure to support the activity and the philosophy. Three data collection methods for monitoring and measuring performance are described, along with the benefits and shortcomings of each. Eight basic data elements that should be captured in the database of any voluntary reporting system are listed. These data collection methods are then applied to each phase of the medication use system to demonstrate their applicability in problem identification and process improvement.

Chapter 3 pulls together the systems approach and the importance of measurement and monitoring presented in the preceding chapters to demonstrate how circumstances can culminate in errors. Real-life cases reported to the U.S. Pharmacopeia Medication Errors Reporting Program show the multidisciplinary and multifaceted attributes of errors. The chapter discusses standardized definitions for "medication error" and types of errors. It discusses how products, processes, and people contribute to medication errors while giving numerous prevention strategies.

Chapter 4 provides definitions of "adverse drug events" and medication errors as "preventable adverse drug events." Specific error prevention strategies are described, for example, in unit dosing, targeted provider education, and computerization and standardization of processes. David Bates describes several real-life examples of system approaches to error reduction, as well as the importance of patient-centered prevention strategies for several settings. The chapter also looks at the not-too distant future when the quality of patient-focused outcomes will depend on computerization to validate accuracy along the medication use continuum and to enable complete information sharing among health care professionals throughout the health care system and its venues.

Chapter 5 provides a practical template for examining your medication use processes, identifying improvements, and taking action. Linda Hanold, Bruce Vinson, and Annette Rubino guide you through the various stages of planning the project, including selecting a team and flowcharting your processes. Performance improvement tools, from brainstorming and multivoting to control charts and scatter diagrams, are explained and applied. Developing the project plan requires careful attention, and the authors suggest that you consider such things as resources, the system's "fit" in your facility's broader vision, and the development of time lines and milestones for reaching your goals.

The final chapter ties together all of the practical and theoretical information given in the first five. It presents a case study of how the Cleveland Clinics Foundation, a 1,000-bed acute care facility, used quality improvement to improve its medication use system. Mardi Atkins and Louis Barone describe numerous safety nets, policies, and protocols instituted by this organization to help avoid errors and prevent recurrence at the various steps in the medication use process. The chapter highlights the organization's nonpunitive, confidential incident reporting system, which tracks medication events, and the method for calculating medication event rates is provided. The case itself describes the introduction of an automated dispensing device and the change in error rates following its installation.

We hope you will find this book useful, practical, and enlightening in your own efforts to improve your medication use system.

Diane DeMichele Cousins
Contributing Editor

Chapter 1:

A SYSTEMS APPROACH TO MEDICATION USE

Deborah M Nadzam, PhD, RN
Vice President, Performance Measurement
Joint Commission on Accreditation of Healthcare Organizations
Oakbrook Terrace, Illinois

rove it. In so many words, users of today's health care system are telling providers and practitioners to demonstrate in quantifiable terms the high quality of care they profess to give consumers. The health care industry is being held accountable for costs and, increasingly, for quality. The public wants to see value for its health care dollar, and, more importantly, it is asking whether care will achieve expected desirable outcomes. At the same time, however, consumers are becoming more aware that unexpected, undesirable outcomes—mistakes—can also happen.

Health care professionals have long known that errors occur during the course of caring for patients. All care processes are vulnerable to error, yet several studies have found that medication-related events are the most frequent type of adverse event.[1-4] The Medical Practice Study, a sentinel study of medical injuries, found that adverse drug events (ADEs) explained 19.4% of all disabling adverse events and that 45% of the ADEs were the result of an error.[5] In two teaching hospitals, Bates et al found that 6.5% of nonobstetrical adults suffered an ADE, 28% of which were due to errors.[2] An analysis of 135 sentinel events evaluated by the Joint Commission

on Accreditation of Healthcare Organizations (Joint Commission) since 1996 reveals that the largest percentage (22%) were related to medication errors. The costs of ADEs have been calculated to include the added cost to hospitalized patients, estimated at $2,000 per ADE,[6] and the costs of malpractice activities, totaling millions of dollars per year for a large hospital. A 1992 summary of litigation costs estimated total annual costs related to medication errors as 220 million dollars.[7]

It is reasonable then to ask, If adverse drug events are such an enormous problem and if health care professionals are aware of this problem, why do errors still occur? Although tremendous efforts have been made to reduce the probability of ADEs, there is still room for improvement. As the health care environment evolves from purely institutional care to community-based services, the opportunities to study events in the aggregate and across settings highlight additional systems issues. With today's health care environment characterized by changes in the boundaries across health care organizations, mergers, acquisitions, closures, changes in the venues where care is provided, and changes in the types

High-Level Portrayal of a Medication Use System

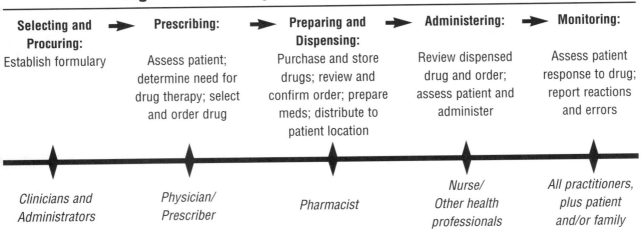

Selecting and Procuring:	Prescribing:	Preparing and Dispensing:	Administering:	Monitoring:
Establish formulary	Assess patient; determine need for drug therapy; select and order drug	Purchase and store drugs; review and confirm order; prepare meds; distribute to patient location	Review dispensed drug and order; assess patient and administer	Assess patient response to drug; report reactions and errors
Clinicians and Administrators	Physician/ Prescriber	Pharmacist	Nurse/ Other health professionals	All practitioners, plus patient and/or family

Figure 1-1. *This flowchart, developed by an expert panel convened by the Joint Commission to define the medication use function, depicts the overall processes involved in the medication use system, and the individuals involved, in an acute care environment.*

of practitioners providing the care, practitioners are now being exposed to the entire continuum of care. The health care industry as a whole is more cognizant of the adverse drug event problem. The occurrence of ADEs, although probably still underreported, is widespread and serious. Attention to preventing ADEs and reducing the frequency of those that do occur has become a priority. Recent analysis of ADEs has begun to focus on a systemwide view. Therefore, we need to look at the total medication use system in order to identify the areas that contribute to ADEs.

This chapter describes medication use as a system; discusses the roles of physicians, pharmacists, nurses, and patients within the system; and describes general approaches for assessing the effectiveness of a medication use system.

Medication Use as a System

A *system* can be defined as a combination of interdependent processes that share a common goal. Medication use within a health care organization can be viewed as a system, with several

components and processes, inputs (patient and drug therapy information), throughputs (care provided), and outputs (effective, efficient, and safe treatment). The provision of medications to patients, regardless of the setting, depends on a set of processes that begins with assessing the patients being cared for—a step that depends on the services provided by the organization. Knowing the patient population will help the organization to determine which drugs it should purchase for patient care. The critical next step involves the individual patient—the assessment of the patient's health status and determination of appropriate drug therapy. Drug preparation and delivery to the patient follow. The patient's response to drug therapy must be monitored to assess the occurrence of desirable and undesirable effects. And finally, ongoing medication therapy management ensures proper dosage, frequency, and integration with other medicines used. Figure 1-1 (above) provides a simpler, high-level depiction of the five core processes in a medication use system.

The availability of over 8,000 drug products[9] is only one variable that provides ample opportunity for errors in the selection, distribution, and administration of medications. Other interacting components that may be present within a single institution include hundreds (thousands in large facilities) of different patients and conditions, hundreds of staff members, different types of practitioners, staff turnover, old and new equipment and technology, and ineffective processes for getting the right drug to the right patient at the right time. In addition, the opportunities for serious ADEs are more common today, given the higher potency of medicines, the increasing number of medications available, the uniqueness of drug delivery systems, and the increasing number of medicines used per patient.

Defining medication use as a system includes identifying the many processes and steps necessary to achieve the function, identifying error-prone steps (risk points), and implementing strategies for preventing or reducing errors. In 1989, the Joint Commission convened an expert panel to define the medication use function and system in the acute care setting and to develop performance measures for monitoring the effectiveness of the function.

The medication use function was defined as "the safe, effective, appropriate, and efficient use of medications." The expert panel then identified four components, or subsystems, of the medication use system:

- Prescribing and selecting the drug for the patient;

- Preparing and dispensing it;

- Administering the drug; and

- Monitoring the patient for effect.

A fifth component, selection and procurement of drugs, was subsequently added.

Within each component, several steps were then identified as necessary for increasing the likelihood that the *right* dose of the *right* drug is provided to the *right* patient through the *right* route at the *right* time with the *right* result (the "Six Rights"). These steps were used to create a detailed flowchart that led to the panel delineating 16 major processes associated with the medication use function (Table 1-1, page 8). An abbreviated flowchart was constructed around these processes (Figure 1-2, page 9). The task force selected the processes depicted on the flowchart because they were believed to be fundamental to an efficient, effective medication use system. In other words, if any of these processes is not operating well, the probability of providing the Six Rights would be diminished.

The left side of the flowchart begins with the patient's admission to a health care organization (originally developed to reflect hospitalization) and determination that drug therapy is indicated. The right side of the chart highlights the hospital's structural components intended to support the clinical function of medication use, including a crossfunctional team, formulary development, and incident and adverse drug reaction reporting systems, each joining the left side of the chart at particular points.

Roles of System Participants

The portrayal in Figure 1-1 of the five core processes in a medication use system emphasizes that the majority of processes in the medication use system occur long before a medication reaches the patient. Thus, there are several steps at which an error can occur and be intercepted before reaching the patient. This diagram also identifies the participants typically associated with each major component and series of steps. Each participant has a slightly different perspective on the Six Rights and a different responsibility in delivering/upholding them.

Table 1-1. Major Processes in the Medication Use Function

Prescribing
- Assessing the need for selecting the correct drug
- Individualizing the therapeutic regimen
- Designating the desired therapeutic response

Dispensing
- Reviewing the order
- Processing the order
- Compounding/preparing the drug
- Dispensing the drug in a timely manner

Administering
- Administering the right medication to the right patient
- Administering the medication when indicated

- Informing the patient about the medication
- Including the patient in administration

Monitoring
- Monitoring and documenting the patient's response
- Identifying and reporting adverse drug reactions or medication errors
- Re-evaluating the drug selection, drug regimen, frequency of administration, and duration

Systems/Management Control
- Collaborating and communicating among caregivers
- Reviewing and managing the patient's complete therapeutic drug regimen

Clinicians and Administrators

Clinicians and administrators are involved in decisions related to the selection, procurement, and storage of drugs. A formulary, which includes drugs necessary to care for the organization's patients, is established. Several types of costs are considered, including purchase prices, storage requirements, and other drug-specific peculiarities (for example, staff education, equipment necessary for administration). The costs associated with medication errors are also important to consider and can be a factor in drug selection.

Prescribers

Historically, prescribing medications has been primarily a physician responsibility, although dentists have also had prescribing privileges. Over the past two decades, other health care professionals have been given prescribing privileges, including psychologists, nurses, and pharmacists. The prescriber wants to ensure that the right drug, dose, and route of administration for the patient's condition is selected, and that the patient will receive the medication at intervals necessary to support effective

and safe physiologic use of the drug. Finally, monitoring the patient's clinical condition to determine the effect of the drug is of prime importance. Has the desired outcome been achieved? Is the patient not responding to the drug or, worse, responding in an undesirable manner?

Pharmacists

Traditionally, other practitioners have perceived the pharmacist's role as simply filling the order correctly—dispensing the right dose of the right drug for the right route and right frequency. "Right" equated to "what the physician intended." Pharmacists today are increasingly recognized for their knowledge of drugs and are expected to question dosages, routes of administration, and frequencies that are unusual for particular drugs, serving as one level of "check" on prescribers. In addition to preparing medications, pharmacists procure and store medications and provide information to other professionals regarding established and new drug therapies. Correct labeling and timely dispensing supports getting the right drug to the right patient at the right time. Fortunately,

Medication Use Flowchart

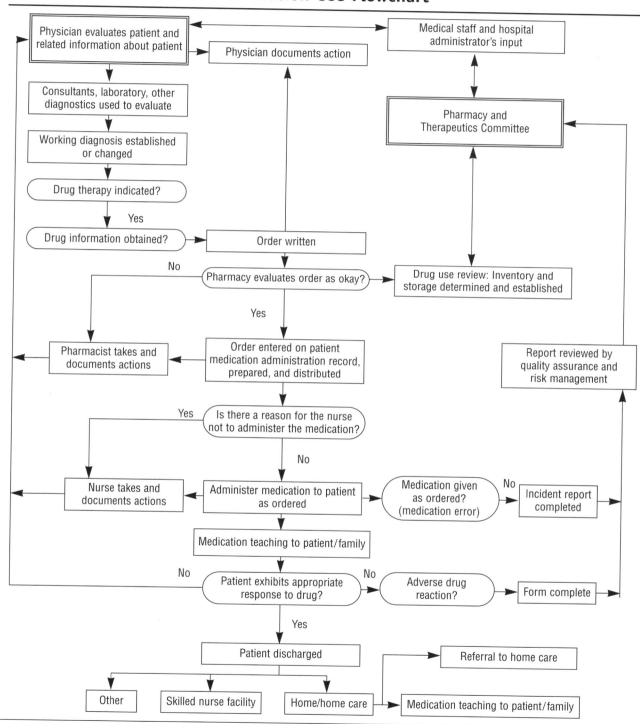

Figure 1–2. *This diagram shows the overall process for the medication use function.*

Source: Joint Commission: New Indicators Target Key Cross-Department Functions. *Joint Commission Perspectives* 9(11/12):7, 1989. Used with permission.

pharmacists have become more involved in the front end of the medication use system. They are participating in decisions related to selection of the right drug for patients, providing pharmacokinetic consultation to prescribers and positively influencing decisions related to selection, dosage, frequency, and route.[11,12] Furthermore, when included on the clinical team, pharmacists also participate in assessing the patient's clinical condition to ascertain and help manage his or her response to drug therapy.

Nurses

It is first important to note that the term *nurse,* when used to describe a direct caregiver, can refer to one of several types of nurses: nurse aides, licensed practical nurses, registered nurses, clinical nurse specialists, and nurse practitioners (the last two are registered nurses with advanced training). Nurse aides do not typically administer medications, although they may certainly be in a position to observe the patient and notice obvious untoward side effects. Licensed practical nurses often deliver medications and are in frequent contact with the patient, again able to note side effects. Registered nurses administer medications and are important members of the medication use team, often noticing less obvious side effects and participating in educating the patient about the medication. Clinical nurse specialists and nurse practitioners may administer and monitor drugs, as well as have prescribing privileges, depending on state law and organization policy.

The Six Rights of medication administration are, or should be, an integral part of nursing education and health care organizations' orientation programs. As with the traditional perspective of pharmacists' duties, "right" has usually meant "what the physician ordered." Within health care organizations, nurses have served as the final check in a series of steps to ensure that the pharmacist prepared and delivered what the prescriber ordered and that the prescriber ordered appropriately. The nurse then assesses the patient to determine whether any change in condition warrants withholding the medication. The nurse, like the pharmacist, is becoming a more active participant in the entire medication use system, often being involved in discussions related to the patient's condition and the need for appropriate drug therapy.

Patients

The final person in the medication use chain is the patient—the recipient of the medication. (Family members or significant others also may be expected to participate in medication administration and monitoring activities, particularly with the growing move toward home care.) Although a patient may recognize a change from a previously received medication, most patients have not questioned different types, numbers, colors, or routes of medication administration. They trust that caregivers are providing necessary treatment according to effective, fail-safe care delivery processes. This behavior is also changing—as well it should. Patient familiarity with medications is increasing as a function of shorter hospital stays and changing patterns related to access to care. Health care professionals should expect and encourage more questions from patients and their caregivers about drug therapy and make them partners in the process.

Importance of Patient Education in Medication Use

The chain of the medication use system comprises many links, yet the chain is only as strong as the weakest link. The expectation to double-check selected, prepared, and dispensed orders and medications is now well understood by prescribers, pharmacists, and nurses. A significant number of medication errors are intercepted before ever reaching the patient, demonstrating the strength of "safety nets" in the process. An interdisciplinary, coordinated approach to improving the medication use system, which includes the patient or caregiver, is necessary to minimize breaks in the chain and maximize results.

The flowchart in Figure 1-2 (page 9) was developed to describe the medication use system in an acute care environment. The same flowchart can be modified to define the medication use function in other settings. It is likely that several processes and steps will be identical or very similar. Even in the community setting, a prescriber determines that drug therapy is indicated and an order must be filled through a pharmacy operation. In some settings, the recipient of medication (patient or consumer) may play a more active role in the actual administration of the medication. As noted earlier, this role underscores the importance of patient education, especially in acute care settings where patients are often discharged with prescribed medications for self-administration. In ambulatory settings and in the home, the patient must have this knowledge from the outset, be prepared to monitor his or her response to the drug, be able to recognize signs of untoward reactions, and know when to notify a health care professional. Although the provision of written information about the medication(s) is helpful, professionals must be sure that the quality of education is sufficient and that the patient has in fact learned the critical information about medication administration and monitoring desired and adverse effects.

Medication Use Systems and Performance Improvement

Proactive and reactive approaches for measuring the performance of a system include identifying measures for continuously monitoring that system, identification of critical steps for which safe-ty nets should be put in place, and a framework for evaluating the root causes contributing to adverse drug events. In non–health care settings such as the nuclear power and airline industries, faulty systems have often been found to be the cause of sentinel events. Although an individual's performance may be identified as the proximate cause of the event, an assessment of the entire system is completed to identify risk points, or weak links, that may have facilitated the individual's less-than-optimal performance. Changes may be made to strengthen the system in order to minimize the risk of another occurrence of the same or a similar event. These industries recognize that training or retraining of personnel also may be necessary if a lack of knowledge is identified as a proximal cause of the error.

In the health care industry, we have typically responded to errors by placing blame on an individual, usually punishing the person in some way, without conducting an assessment of the system as a whole. This type of response has only served to decrease voluntary reporting of errors and limit opportunities for studying the system as a whole. Without aggregate data about errors, the inefficiency and ineffectiveness of a system cannot be identified and improved. In fact, this approach only perpetuates a dangerous assumption that the system works well and the individual is the only problem.

Root Cause Analysis

Root cause analysis is a process for identifying the basic or causal factor(s) that underlie variation in performance, including the occurrence or possible occurrence of a sentinel event. Most frequently, the technique is used reactively—to probe the reason for problems that have already occurred. The process is then used to identify the most obvious opportunities for improvement that will prevent recurrence. However, root cause analysis may also be used proactively to even greater organizational benefit to study processes in order to prevent future problems from ever occurring.

Root cause analysis helps organizations look underneath the apparent or proximate causes to get at the root(s) of an event. Root cause analysis has the following characteristics:

- It focuses primarily on systems and processes, not individual performance;

- It progresses from special causes in clinical processes to common causes in organizational processes;

- It repeatedly digs deeper by asking "Why?" until no additional logical answer can be identified; and

- It identifies changes that could be made in systems and processes—through either redesign or development of new systems or processes—that would improve the level of performance and reduce the risk of a particular serious sentinel event occurring in the future.

With root cause analysis, the focus is not punitive. Rather, it is on systems—on how to improve systems in order to prevent the occurrence of sentinel events. The approach involves digging into the organization's systems to find new ways to do things. It is focused on answering the question, "What should we *do* to prevent this in the future?" not "What should we *have done* to prevent this from having occurred?" The rush to point a finger at someone who can be blamed for a problem is not a part of this process. Rather, a problem is perceived as everyone's problem and everyone's challenge to fix or improve. The emphasis is on improving systems of which clinical processes and people are but a part.

For example, human error by a physician prescribing a drug or by a nurse administering one may be the proximate cause of a patient's death. When practitioners receive information alerting them to medications that lead to adverse drug-drug interactions, for example, they may be able to remember the adverse interactions for the drugs they most frequently prescribe. However, the increasing number of drugs, the large number of possible drug-drug interactions, and the constantly expanding knowledge base in this area make it all but impossible for individuals to remember all the possible interactions. Errors in memory will and do occur even with the best-intentioned and most competent human beings.

Drug prescribing and administration processes are likely to be improved only when they are seen as part of the larger medication-use system that involves physicians, the pharmacy, nurses, and information management staff. Therefore, implementation of a new process geared to preventing a future error in prescribing or administering a drug would be of benefit. Perhaps the information management staff could install a computer-based ordering system linked to a real-time expert system. This would provide on-line feedback to the physician about potential adverse drug-drug interactions, thereby permitting better-informed clinical judgment. Or perhaps the pharmacy staff could install a unit-dose drug-distribution system to assist the nurses in drug administration. These changes do not send a signal that the pharmacy and information services staff were negligent or to blame for the error. Rather, these staffs are in a position to change the design of the organization's information management system to reduce future special-cause variations in clinical processes.

Success with root cause analysis is founded on the belief that humans make mistakes and errors are inevitable, but that organizational improvement is always possible and the ever-present goal. Root cause analysis has the highest potential for success in environments or organizational cultures where individuals are not afraid to report errors. Punishment effectively alters or stifles the necessary climate. The organization's leaders need to be committed both to limiting individual blame and punishment and to the root cause analysis process as an effective way to identify improvement opportunities.

General Recommendations for Improving the Medication Use System

Several organizations, researchers, and clinicians have already identified general strategies for improving medication use within health care settings. They include

- protocols, guidelines, policies, and reporting systems;

- proactive approaches for improving the system and preventing errors; and

- reactive strategies for understanding how errors have occurred.

A brief review of these strategies is given here; Chapter 4 provides specific details on these and additional strategies.

Developing Protocols, Guidelines, Policies, and Reporting Systems

One strategy for maximizing the effectiveness and efficiency of the medication use function within a health care organization is to implement particular protocols, guidelines, and policies. Orienting staff members to and holding them accountable for following organizational procedures encourages the use of protocols. Protocols may be developed within the organization; standards of care and practice are available from professional organizations. Protocols and guidelines for particular drugs also are available in the literature and from pharmaceutical companies, making it unnecessary to reinvent such procedures.

Building an effective system for reporting adverse drug events also supports an effective medication use system. Improving the medication use system depends on knowing where the weak links are. Weak links can be identified if system failures—errors—are reported or anticipated.

There is general agreement that the majority of medication errors go unreported. Errors can be detected through voluntary self-reporting, incident reporting, or direct observation techniques (discussed in Chapter 2).[13] Computer screening, chart review, and incident reports are some methods to report discovered errors. However, if an error is not discovered or if the staff member involved is fearful of retribution, an error may go unreported. Day and colleagues found that nurses were not always sure what constituted an error.[14] In addition, they complained about the complex, time-consuming process associated with completing a report. The negative connotation of the term *error* and fear of punishment also contributed to failure to report recognized errors.

Proactive Approaches

Proactive strategies for improving the medication use system include ongoing monitoring of the system and implementation of specific structures, policies, and procedures. An example of the former would be the use of performance measures. Using the 16 processes from Table 1-1 as a base, the expert panel convened by the Joint Commission developed specific indicators or performance measures for use in assessing the performance of the medication use system as a whole. Following two phases of field testing, five medication use measures were included in the Joint Commission's performance measurement system, the Indicator Measurement System™ (IMSystem™). One of the five measures actually has four different rates for four different drugs, making the total number of available

Table 1-2. Medication Use Indicators Included in the IMSystem™

Indicator Statement	Intent and Rationale of Indicator
Inpatients 65 years of age or older in whom creatinine clearance has been estimated or measured	The intent of this indicator is to monitor the process of individualizing medication dosage by focusing on a group of patients susceptible to dose-related toxicity. Older patients are more prone to changes in renal function with aging. These changes can be a cause of dose-related drug toxicity. Creatinine clearance is an important gauge of the patient's ability to excrete drugs that can become toxic in high concentrations. Estimated creatinine clearance is an acceptable substitute for the actual creatinine clearance measurement if appropriate formulas are used.
Selected surgical procedures for which prophylactic intravenous antibiotics were received: timing of prophylactic antibiotic administration	The intent of this indicator is to monitor the timeliness of antibiotic administration used to prevent surgical site infections. An essential principle of antibiotic prophylaxis is the achievement of adequate antibiotic serum and tissue concentrations prior to the surgical incision and throughout the procedure. The period immediately prior to surgical incision is considered the optimum time for administration of these antibiotics to reduce the risk of surgery-related infection.
Inpatients with a discharge diagnosis of insulin dependent diabetes mellitus who demonstrate self blood glucose monitoring and self administration of insulin before discharge, or are referred for post-discharge follow-up for diabetes management	The intent of this indicator is to assess the process of informing and educating the patient about proper medication use. The measure is designed to serve as an index of the effectiveness of patient education regarding medication use by monitoring a specific population of patients known to require extensive medication teaching.
Inpatients receiving digoxin who have no corresponding measured drug level or whose highest measured level exceeds a specific limit	This indicator is designed to evaluate the process of monitoring the patient's response to drug therapy, with a drug where failure to maintain levels within acceptable therapeutic ranges can have significant adverse clinical consequences. A serum digoxin level exceeding 3.0 mg/mL places the patient in the numerator.

(continued on page 15)

Table 1-2. Medication Use Indicators Included in the IMSystem™ *(continued)*

Indicator Statement	Intent and Rationale of Indicator
Inpatients receiving theophylline who have no corresponding measured drug level or whose highest measured level exceeds a specific limit	This indicator is designed to evaluate the process of monitoring the patient's response to drug therapy, with a drug where failure to maintain levels within acceptable therapeutic ranges can have significant adverse clinical consequences. A serum theophylline level exceeding 15 mcg/mL in patients less than 28 days old, or 20 mcg/mL in other patients places the patient in the numerator.
Inpatients receiving phenytoin who have no corresponding measured drug level or whose highest measured level exceeds a specific limit	This indicator is designed to evaluate the process of monitoring the patient's response to drug therapy, with a drug where failure to maintain levels within acceptable therapeutic ranges can have significant adverse clinical consequences. A serum phenytoin level exceeding 15 mcg/mL in patients less than 28 days old, or 20 mcg/mL in other patients places the patient in the numerator.
Inpatients receiving lithium who have no corresponding measured drug level or whose highest measured level exceeds a specific limit	This indicator is designed to evaluate the process of monitoring the patient's response to drug therapy, with a drug where failure to maintain levels within acceptable therapeutic ranges can have significant adverse clinical consequences. A serum lithium level exceeding 1.5 mEq/L places the patient in the numerator.
Inpatients' number of prescribed medications at discharge	This is a continuous-variable indicator and is designed to direct attention to the need for review of the patient's drug regimen at key junctures. Several studies have found that adverse drug events and medication noncompliance are highly correlated with the number of medications taken. Note: this indicator counts the number of prescribed medications, not the number of prescriptions.

measures eight. These measures address prescribing, distributing, administering, and monitoring of medications. Table 1-2 (pages 14 and above) lists the indicator statements for these measures and describes the intent of each in relation to the medication use system as a whole, for example, assessing patient education or monitoring patient response.

Analysis of data collected proactively, such as through the use of performance measures, can help identify process improvement opportunities. For example, ongoing monitoring of diabetic patients' ability to self-administer insulin and monitor blood glucose levels may reveal that medication teaching efforts are not achieving desired results or are overlooking part of the

Table 1-3. Ten Guidelines to Develop a Solid Game Plan for Avoiding Medication Errors

1. Use automated dispensing systems safely.
2. Stop storing dangerous drugs in clinical areas.
3. Correct poor practice habits.
4. Steer clear of communication breakdowns.
5. Use quality assurance methods to reduce errors.
6. Decrease access to the pharmacy for nonpharmacy personnel.
7. Make important clinical information available when and where it's needed.
8. Encourage manufacturers to evaluate drug brand names, labeling, and packaging before introducing new products.
9. Focus most on patient care, not cost.
10. Turn medication errors into pearls of wisdom.

Source: Adapted from Cohen MR, Cohen HG. Medication errors: Following a game plan for continued improvement. *Nursing* 26(11):34–37, Nov 1996.

identified population. Actions to improve this process should then be taken.

Several other authors and professional groups have also suggested steps for improving medication use within health care organizations. Seven high-priority actions for preventing adverse drug events in hospitals were proposed by an expert panel convened by the American Society of Health-System Pharmacists (discussed in Chapter 4). Cohen and Cohen also offer ten guidelines for avoiding medication errors (Table 1-3, above). Additional strategies are addressed in other chapters of this book.

Reactive Strategies
Perhaps the most familiar approach to medication system improvement is reacting to medication errors. A hallmark study of a systems analysis of adverse drug events was conducted by Leape and colleagues.[15] The investigators classified 247 ADEs and 194 potential ADEs by type of error (according to major components within the system) and proximal causes. An *adverse drug event* was defined as "an injury resulting from medical intervention related to a drug."[2] *Potential adverse drug events* were defined as "errors that have the capacity to cause injury, but fail to do so, either by chance or because they are intercepted."[1] *Proximal cause* was defined as the apparent "reason" the error was made and included such things as lack of knowledge of the drug, lack of information about the patient, transcription error, faulty dose checking, preparation errors, and others. Proximal causes were then dissected to identify system failures that allowed the causes to exist. Such failures included ineffective dissemination of drug information, lack of availability of patient information, manual transcription processes and illegible handwriting, poor communication between different services, preparation of intravenous medication by nurses, and inadequate staffing.

Leape and his colleagues proposed a framework of "Third Order Why's"[15] to highlight system ineffectiveness within a facility. First, ask why the incident occurred (What was the error?). Second, ask why the error occurred (What was the proximal cause?). Third, ask why the proximal cause occurred (What were the underlying system failures?). This approach may be helpful when evaluating a sentinel event or when conducting a more intense evaluation to understand other performance measurement data.

Systems Working Together
A health care organization comprises several systems, of which the medication use system is just one. It is a system that tends to affect all patients, all services, many departments, and many health care professionals throughout the continuum of care. In addition, it can affect and be affected by other systems. An efficient system for admitting a

patient and determining treatment needs can make the difference between timely, efficacious drug therapy and "too little, too late" scenarios.

Drug therapy affects more patients than any other type of medical treatment. As a result, health care providers are committed to the safe and effective use of medications. Defining errors, reporting errors, proactive monitoring of performance, and continuous improvement will help to ensure that a high quality of care is provided to the public. Chapter 2 discusses ways of looking at the processes involved in medication use systems to identify opportunities for improvement.

References

1. Leape LL, Brennan TA, Laird N, et al: The nature of adverse events in hospitalized patients: Results of the Harvard Medical Practice Study II. *N Engl J Med* 324(6):377–384, 1991.

2. Bates DW, Cullen DJ, Laird N, et al: Incidence of adverse drug events and potential adverse drug events. *JAMA* 274(1):29–34, 1996.

3. Allan EL, Barker KN: Fundamentals of medication error research. *Am J Hosp Pharm* 47(3):555–571, 1990.

4. National Association of Insurance Commissioners: *Medical Malpractice Closed Claims, 1975–1978.* Brookfield, WI: National Association of Insurance Commissioners, 1980.

5. Leape LL, Lawthers AG, Brennan TA, Johnson WG: Preventing medical injury. *Qual Rev Bull* 19:144–149, 1993.

6. Evans RS, Classen DC, Stevens LE, et al: Using a hospital information system to assess the effects of adverse drug events. *Proc Annu Symp Comput Appl Med Care* 17:161–65, 1993.

7. Medication errors: High liability and price for hospitals. *Hosp Risk Manage* 14(10):129–33, 1992.

8. Berrien FK: *General and Social Systems.* New York: Rutgers University Press, 1968.

9. Pepper G: Errors in drug administration by nurses. *Am J Health Syst Pharm* 52(4):390–395, 1995.

10. Nadzam DM: Development of medication-use indicators by the Joint Commission on Accreditation of Healthcare Organizations. *Am J Hosp Pharm* 48(9):1925–1930, 1991.

11. Avorn J: Putting adverse drug events into perspective. Editorial. *JAMA* 277(4):341–342, 1997.

12. Morlock C: Pharmacist involvement in home care practice. *U.S. Pharmacist.* July: 5–10, 1997.

13. Van Leeuwen DH: Are medication error rates useful as comparative measures of organizational performance? *Jt Comm J Qual Improv* 20(4):192–199, 1994.

14. Day G, Hindmarsh J, Hojna C, Roy G, Ventimiglia N: Improving medication administration through an enhanced occurrence reporting system. *J Nurs Care Qual* 9(1):51–56, 1994.

15. Leape LL, Bates DW, Cullen DJ, et al: Systems analysis of adverse drug events. *JAMA* 274(1):35–43, 1995.

Chapter 2

MEASURING AND MONITORING THE PERFORMANCE OF THE MEDICATION USE SYSTEM

Philip J Schneider, RPh, MS
Director, Latiolais Leadership Program
Clinical Professor, College of Pharmacy
The Ohio State University
Columbus, Ohio

Maja Gift, RPh
Interim Director of Pharmacy
Pharmacotherapy Specialist, Quality Improvement/Outcomes
Tampa General Healthcare
Tampa, Florida

In the previous chapter, the importance of a systems approach to medication use was discussed. This chapter explains the rationale for and the techniques used to measure and monitor the performance of the processes that make up the medication use system. The goals of examining process performance are to

- identify problem-prone components that need improvement,

- test ideas that might reduce medication errors, and

- track performance to see whether implementing new ideas improves medication use.

Most organizations do not take a systematic approach to monitoring the performance of medication use processes. There may be components of a performance measurement process in place, but establishment of baseline performance, tracking of the impact of improvement strategies, and

multidisciplinary review of information are rarely done. As a result, the performance of medication use processes is not accurately measured, improvement strategies are not evaluated, the multidisciplinary approach needed to improve the processes is not achieved, and the processes cannot be continuously improved.

Virtually all patients in a health care system receive medications. The system by which drug treatment decisions are made is complex, interdisciplinary, problem prone, and high risk. The medication use system consists of five processes:

- Selecting and procuring (systems/management control);

- Prescribing;

- Preparing and dispensing;

- Administering; and

- Monitoring.

Although each process is often associated with a specific health care professional or discipline, in reality, each may be performed by various participants in the process—physicians, pharmacists, nurses, clerks, physical therapists, radiology technicians, respiratory technologists, or the patient—depending on the setting or circumstances. The performance of the entire system depends on all of these professionals and patients working together to optimize the performance of the medication use processes and to minimize the occurrence of medication errors.

Measurement Framework

The purpose of measuring any process is to evaluate its performance and assess the impact of changes in procedures on performance. In virtually all cases, the intent is to continually improve and optimize the performance of the process. In the case of medication use, the purpose is to safely provide medications to patients by reducing the chances of medication errors and preventable adverse drug events.

The first step in establishing a good measurement system is to make measuring medication use processes a priority in the organization. The choice of what to measure is guided by organization needs and logistics. If a medication error program or adverse drug reaction program is already in place, it may be best to use this program and concentrate on improving reporting rates and developing a relational database to analyze the data. Many existing programs need improvement so that meaningful information can be obtained. If the institution is aware of quality issues that need to be addressed, focused studies or other programs will need to be considered. For example, if a significant or catastrophic error has occurred, a root cause analysis should be performed (discussed in Chapter 1) and a recommendation

for ongoing monitoring of a process component may be necessary.

Next, staff should be assigned the responsibility of measuring and monitoring the performance of medication use processes by developing a measurement system and analyzing the data produced by the system. This responsibility is often assigned to a single individual, such as a pharmacist, nurse, or risk manager, but it also may be assigned to a multidisciplinary group, such as a pharmacy and therapeutics committee or a medication use process improvement team. The group method can be beneficial because medication use is multidisciplinary and almost all patient care providers participate in a medication use process to some degree. To effect change and improve the process, representatives from many disciplines need to be involved and prepared to change behavior. The group should be responsible for developing the measurement programs, reviewing and analyzing information, and recommending policy changes to improve the medication use system. It should also be expected to document improvement when changes are made. As a multidisciplinary team, it should be process based and not focus on the parochial agendas of individual departments or disciplines.

The next step is to generate organization commitment to improving the performance of medication use processes. An important element in averting the fear of potential liability associated with reporting and review of medication errors is to make sure that process measurement information is nondiscoverable, that is, that it will not be used for any purpose other than quality improvement. This information also cannot be used for disciplinary action or individual performance appraisals.

After an infrastructure is established and before the group begins to measure and monitor the performance of the medication use process, the data elements that will be used to track performance need to be determined. Specifics on selecting these data elements are discussed in the following section. After selecting the data elements, staff members need to be trained to collect the data. Who will need training depends on the type(s) of data to be collected. For example, if voluntary incident reports will be used, all staff members who provide direct patient care need to be trained and motivated to prepare and submit reports. On the other hand, if observation-based data collection will be used, the observers will need to be trained to gather data that are complete, but to do so in an unobtrusive, unbiased way so as not to modify ordinary performance. Rare events, such as deaths caused by medication errors, are difficult to identify using sampling-based observation techniques. Usually voluntary reporting systems, such as incident reports, are more suited to identifying serious, infrequent events. Voluntary reporting and observation-based data collection methods are discussed in greater detail in the next section.

The Data Collection Process

The key to performance measurement and improvement is collecting and comparing data over a defined time interval. Several types of data can be collected and compared to measure and monitor the performance of medication use. Some examples include the following:

- Interventions when physician orders need to be clarified or corrected;

- Drug use evaluation studies that evaluate prescribing and monitoring of high-volume, problem-prone, high-risk drugs;

- Errors detected when checking medications before they are dispensed;

- Sterility testing of intravenous (IV) admixture medications;

- Medication errors documented by incident reports;

- Medication errors detected by observation of persons administering drugs;

- Dispensing records that show whether patients received medications as prescribed; and

- Adverse reactions to medications after they have been administered to patients.

Health care organizations have collected all of these types of data; many have reported their findings in the literature. Such documentation is even required by Joint Commission accreditation standards. In many cases, information is underreported, not tracked and trended over time, not reviewed by appropriate persons or committees, or not acted on when it *is* reviewed. If the information is collected, it is not usually compared to "best practice" standards to measure performance (benchmarking). Thus, opportunities to improve the processes are wasted. It is likely that most organized health care systems, particularly hospitals, already have many— if not all—of these data systems in place. They often do not use the information properly to identify opportunities for process improvement.

Qualitative Versus Quantitative Measurement

One of the traps in measuring process performance is choosing to focus on quantitative data and undervaluing qualitative results. Organizations often attempt to identify a performance indicator that produces a single number to reflect service quality. For example, an organization might try to track its medication error rate as one indicator of the quality of patient care. To quantitatively measure the incidence of medication errors and produce an accurate analysis, the organization would need to conduct a time-consuming, observation-based study on a regular basis. Medication errors are underreported with a voluntary reporting system compared to an observation-based system. Nevertheless, useful information can be generated inexpensively by evaluating voluntary error reports over time to find aspects of the medication use system (steps in a process, certain drugs, areas of the system, or times in the day) where errors are more common and corrective actions are needed. Indeed, aggregate voluntary reports provide a "semiquantitative" measure of performance. Large changes (whether good or bad) in commonly reported errors can reflect similar changes in performance. Also, a few serious events found through a voluntary reporting program can be as useful and more timely than information produced in an observation-based study. Thus, care needs to be used in balancing the need for quantitative information versus qualitative or semiquantitative information. Both have their place, but qualitative information is usually easier to collect and more useful for quality improvement efforts.

Data Collection Methods

There are three general methods for collecting data to monitor and measure the performance of medication use processes: observation-based studies, voluntary reporting programs, and criteria-based audits.

Observation-based studies. These are scientifically valid studies based on actual observation of events that document frequency of occurrence. Examples of observation-based studies are unit-dose cart checks and observation-based medication error studies that measure deviations between prescribing orders and drug administration, not the performance of the prescribing process itself. The advantage of observation-based studies is that they accurately reflect actual practice. Such studies do not rely on the initiative of staff members to prepare and submit accurate voluntary reports.

Observation-based studies have the disadvantage of being labor intensive, expensive, and time consuming, and they usually do not detect rare events. In fact, most observed medication errors are not significant and do not result in clinical consequences. Although this method may identify weaknesses in the system, the errors it captures are often dismissed as trivial and of insufficient significance to warrant organization changes.

As noted earlier, an important aspect of observation-based studies is selecting a sample size and sampling technique that ensure a scientifically valid evaluation of the performance of medication use processes. It is important to use an adequate sample size so as to generate scientifically valid results. In some cases, all events should be observed. For example, in the dispensing process, it is legally required that all doses not dispensed by a pharmacist be checked by a pharmacist, a procedure that is easily validated. When observation-based data collection is used, sample size needs to be determined. For some elements of the process, all identified events, such as unit-dose cart filling errors, should be investigated. Other events that are more prevalent require that a statistically valid sample size and sampling method be used so the results of a limited number of observations can be extrapolated to an overall incidence rate. It would not make sense to evaluate only one patient care area or shift. In the drug administration process, for example, it would be impractical to observe all drug administration events because literally millions of doses are administered each year in a large organization.

Data collection needs to be representative. Sample sizes are usually determined based on the expected frequency of events. The more common the anticipated event, the smaller the sample size needed to determine how often it actually happens. The following assumptions need to be made when determining sample size:

Latin Square Design

	Week #1	Week #2	Week #3	Week #4	Week #5
Monday	7th floor	8th floor	9th floor	10th floor	11th floor
Tuesday	8th floor	9th floor	10th floor	11th floor	7th floor
Wednesday	9th floor	10th floor	11th floor	7th floor	8th floor
Thursday	10th floor	11th floor	7th floor	8th floor	9th floor
Friday	11th floor	7th floor	8th floor	9th floor	10th floor

Figure 2-1. *The Latin square design ensures representative sampling for all locations by checking practice on different floors on different days during each week of the study.*

Source: Kirk RE: *Experimental Design: Procedures for the Behavioral Sciences*, 2nd ed. Pacific Grove, CA: Brooks-Cole Publishing Co, 1982, pp 308. Used with permission of the publisher.

1. Confidence interval (z). It is standard to use the 95% confidence interval. This means that there is a 95% chance that the observed results reflect the actual case. In statistical formulas, the confidence interval is specified by the value selected for z. A z value of 2 specifies a 95% confidence interval.

2. Precision (H). This is the range that is acceptable for data. For example, a precision of 2% means that the results are accurate in a range of ± 2%, making a range of 3% to 7% acceptable for an error rate of 5%.

3. Expected error rate (π). Calculating a sample size requires that the error rate expected be estimated. Medication error rates in the typical hospital have been reported to range between 5% and 10%.

The formula for calculating sample size[1] based on these three assumptions is:

$$n = [z^2/H^2] \, (\pi) \, (1 - \pi)$$

where:

n = sample size;

z = confidence interval;

H = precision; and

π = proportion of errors.

For example, an organization wants to perform an observation-based study of drug administration errors. The assumption is made that a 10% error rate ($\pi = 0.1$) exists. It is decided to do a study that results in data with a 95% confidence interval ($z = 2$) and a precision of 2% ($H = 0.02$). Using the formula, the results would be as follows:

$$n = [z^2/H^2](\pi) \, (1 - \pi)$$
$$= [(2)^2/(0.02)^2] \, (0.1) \, (1 - 0.1)$$
$$= [4/0.0004] \, (0.1) \, (0.9)$$
$$= 900 \text{ observations}$$

Sampling technique should ensure that representative observations are made in all areas of the organization. This involves assigning observers to evaluate the drug administration process in different sites on different days. A Latin square design, such as the one shown in Figure 2-1 (above), can be used to achieve this representative sampling.[2]

The use of disguised versus nondisguised observers has been debated. The impact of a change in environment (such as the presence of an observer) on performance has been documented and is known as the Hawthorne effect. Disguising observers is difficult, however, given the number of observations and sites where data are collected. For these reasons, in spite of the potential for the Hawthorne effect, most investigators do not disguise data collectors, assuming that they do not significantly affect the performance of persons administering medications.

To avoid bias and ethical dilemmas, observers record the drug administration event on a data collection form, without being aware of the correct dose, route of administration, or regimen. The accuracy of the administration is determined later by comparing the observation to the drug order. Drug administration records also are reviewed (after the review of drug orders) to identify drugs ordered but not administered (errors of omission). Allan and Barker comprehensively cover the fundamentals of medication error research and observation-based studies.[3]

Voluntary reporting programs. These are programs in which staff members are asked to voluntarily report events that occur and are observed in practice. These reports are then entered into a database that can summarize the experiences and identify trends over time. An example of a voluntary reporting program is incident report-based medication error reporting. Voluntary reporting programs can be specific to an individual health care organization or national as with the United States Pharmacopeia (USP) Medication Error Reporting Program or the Food and Drug Administration (FDA) MedWatch program.*

Voluntary reporting programs have the advantages of being less time consuming than other methods, of getting staff members involved in quality improvement efforts and of being able to detect rare events. National voluntary reporting programs can detect more events than an individual institution, including very infrequent but serious errors.

The disadvantages of this method are that the programs are not completely quantitative and the rate of reporting depends on the motivation of the staff. Underreporting can result when each person involved in an event thinks the other will report it. Some may not want to be perceived as blaming others for a mistake or fear repercussion from peers or employers. The reports may potentially be used for punitive purposes if the organization is not committed to quality improvement at all levels. An anonymous reporting system may be used to avoid any risk of assigning blame, but a disadvantage of such a system is that once the report is filed, it is impossible to get more information. Often these reports lack the details needed to find out what really happened. Therefore, it is more desirable to avoid using voluntary reports for disciplinary purposes and employ them strictly for quality improvement purposes. Effective voluntary reporting programs require eliminating the "culture of fear," and there are several good references on how to approach this.[4,5]

The success of voluntary reporting systems is often assessed by measuring the number of reports per unit of time. Leaders need to recognize that high numbers of reports are not a reflection of poorly performing systems, but opportunities for process improvement. Low reporting rates may be a sign of ineffective reporting rather than good performance. The way that errors are defined also affects reporting rates. Without an organized approach and organizationwide commitment, only a few medication errors will be reported voluntarily. The number of reports needed to effectively evaluate medication use processes has not been researched. Voluntary reporting rates of 300 per month for errors in prescribing and 150 per month for drug administration errors are possible in a large organization through active pro-

---

* Reports of medication errors can be made confidentially by telephone either to the USP (1-800-23ERROR) or to the MedWatch program (1-800-FDA-1088).

motion of the program, sharing successes in process improvement, and attempting to drive out fear of reporting. It is widely agreed that even these numbers reflect significant underreporting (as low as 10%) of the true rates of these events.

Criteria-based audits. These are reviews of practices judged against predefined quality performance standards. An example of a criteria-based audit is medication use evaluation. Medication use evaluation is "a performance improvement method that focuses on evaluating and improving the medication use process with the goal of optimal patient outcomes . . . and may be applied to a medication, therapeutic class disease state or condition, a medication use process (prescribing, dispensing, administering and monitoring), or specific outcomes."[6] An excellent summary of medication use evaluation is given in the American Society of Health-System Pharmacists' guideline on medication use evaluation.[7] The most important steps in medication use evaluation are

- establishing criteria, guidelines, treatment protocols, and standards of care for specific medications or the medication use system based on scientific evidence from the literature;

- educating health care professionals to promote the use of the criteria, guidelines, treatment protocols, and standards of care;

- initiating the use of these criteria to evaluate the use of medications;

- collecting data and evaluating care;

- developing and implementing plans for improvement based on deviations from the criteria;

- assessing the effectiveness of the actions taken;

- incorporating improvements into the criteria, guidelines, treatment protocols, and standards of care; and

- repeating the cycle.

Medications that may be selected for evaluation include the following:

- Medications known to cause adverse drug events (possibly based on information from voluntary reports);

- Medications used for high-risk patients;

- Commonly used medications;

- Medications that are a critical component of care;

- Potentially toxic medications; and

- Medications that are more effective when used in a particular way.

Data collection methods may involve chart review or more efficient computerized screening systems.

Criteria-based audits have the advantage of selectively focusing on a potential problem area and are quantitative evaluations of performance in a targeted area of practice. The disadvantages of such audits are that they are time consuming and labor intensive to perform, and the criteria or guidelines used to evaluate practice require approval in advance of data collection.

Use of Collected Data
Regardless of the method of collection, data need to be analyzed and put into an understandable format to create usable information. Relational databases are an excellent way to do this. To use relational databases effectively, the important aspects of each event need to be defined. Examples of important aspects of analyzing medication errors include

- drug name;

- therapeutic category;

- error type;

- proximal cause/process failure;

- outcome/severity;

- location of patient;

- service involved; and

- stage of medication use system at which the error occurred.

The proximal cause of the error, sometimes referred to as the process failure, is frequently the most useful data element in evaluating system failures and designing improvement strategies. For example, if an inappropriately high dose of renally excreted medication is prescribed and administered to a patient with compromised renal function, the error is categorized as follows: The error type is "wrong dose" and the cause of the error is lack of information about the patient's renal function. There is a degree of subjectivity associated with assigning a cause to errors reported through a voluntary reporting system. The group of practitioners responsible for tracking and reviewing medication errors can minimize the degree of subjective judgment involved by developing definitions that are specific to the organization. If controversy occurs, a group consensus technique can be employed.

An example of a reporting and assessment tool is shown in Figure 2-2, page 27. This document lists the types of errors to be reported, possible proximal causes, and possible outcomes. Data from this form are used to enter information about each medication error reported into a relational database. Reports can then be generated for review based on any specified set of criteria, for example, all errors related to insulin.

Severity ranking is often an important aspect of adverse drug event databases because it permits identification of the most severe errors for review. Usually improvements are needed most when

errors cause serious clinical consequences. It may take too much time to review the details of all errors on a routine basis. It may be more useful to focus case reviews regularly on errors that result in increases in length of stay, transfer to the intensive care unit, permanent harm, or death. Common errors that do not result in clinical consequences or only result in a need for increased monitoring may not need to be reviewed as frequently. Errors can be sorted by severity using a relational database and a severity scale[8-10] such as the one shown in Table 2-1 (page 28). A similar system for categorizing medication errors by outcome, the Medication Error Index, was recently developed by the National Coordinating Council for Medication Error Reporting and Prevention and was adopted July 16, 1996 (Table 2-2, page 29).

An obvious strategy in process improvement is comparing organization performance to outside "best performers," or *benchmarking*. Unfortunately, so few organizations use standardized, quantitative information that benchmarking the performance of medication use processes is virtually impossible. It is possible to create benchmarks within an organization by setting aggressive but achievable goals and measuring performance over time. An improvement model based on this concept has been described by Langley and Nolan.[11] The *internal benchmark* model involves asking three fundamental questions:

- *Aim: What are we trying to accomplish?* It is important to set the internal benchmarks against which process performance will be compared. For example, an aim might be to administer parenteral antibiotics within 60 minutes of the treatment decision.

- *Current knowledge: How will we know that a change is an improvement?* A measurement system must be developed to assess baseline performance and to see whether making changes improves perfor-

Medication Error Reporting and Assessment Tool

CONFIDENTIAL
THE OHIO STATE UNIVERSITY MEDICAL CENTER ADVERSE DRUG EVENT ASSESSMENT TOOLS

Type of ADE:

___ preventable ADE   ___ non-preventable ADE   ___ non-intercepted potential ADE   ___ intercepted potential ADE

Type of Error
(Circle one)

A   Missed dose
B   Wrong dose
C   Wrong drug
D   Known allergy
E   Wrong choice
F   Wrong time
G   Wrong frequency
H   Wrong technique
I   Wrong route
J   Drug–drug interaction
K   Extra dose
L   Failure to act on feet
M   Wrong patient
N   Inadequate monitoring
O   Preparation error
P   Wrong IV solution
Q   Unauthorized drug
R   Wrong rate
S   Contaminated/outdated drug

Proximal Cause
(Circle one)

A   Lack of knowledge about the drug
B   Lack of information about the patient
C   Rule violations
D   Slip or memory lapses
E   Transcription error
F   Faulty drug identity checking
G   Faulty interaction with other services
H   Faulty dose checking
I   Inadequate monitoring
J   Infusion pump mechanical
K   Infusion pump programming
L   Free flow
M   Stocking/delivery problems
N   Preparation errors
O   Lack of standardization
P   Faulty patient identity checking

Outcome

A   Increased monitoring   YES   NO
    needed?
B   Vital signs changes?   YES   NO
C   Additional lab work   YES   NO
    ordered?
D   Additional procedures   YES   NO
    ordered?
E   Treatment needed?   YES   NO
F   Transfer to ICU?   YES   NO

Location: _____
Medical Division: _____
MD: _____

Date: _____
MR # _____
Assigned Cause # _____
Severity Ranking _____
Drug Class _____

Drug _____
Drug 2 _____

Stage of Medication Use Process

PO Physician ordering
TV Transcription verification
PD Pharmacy dispensing/delivery
NA Nurse administration
ME Monitoring of effects

Severity*

A Fatal/life threatening
B Serious
C Significant
D Clinically insignificant

* Prefix with A if actual and P if potential

System Failure

1. Drug knowledge dissemination
2. Dose and identity checking
3. Patient information availability
4. Order transcription
5. Allergy defense system
6. Medication order tracking
7. Interservice communication
8. Device use

9. Standardization of doses and frequencies
10. Preparation of IV medications by nurses
11. Transfer/transition procedures
12. Conflict resolution
13. Staffing work assignments
14. Standardization of procedures
15. Standardization of drug distribution
16. Feedback about adverse drug events

Figure 2-2. *This form includes several of the important aspects needed to analyze medication errors, including the type of error that occurred, its proximal cause, the outcome, the stage at which the error occurred, and what type of system failure is indicated. ADE, adverse drug event; IV, intravenous; MR, medical record.*

Source: The Ohio State University Medical Center, Columbus. Used with permission.

Table 2-1. The Ohio State University Severity Scale

Severity Level	Description
0	Errors intercepted before they reach the patient
1	No change in clinical outcome
2	Increased monitoring required
3	Additional laboratory tests or change in vital signs
4	Treatment or procedure required, increased length of stay, or hospital (re)admission
5	Transfer to intensive care unit, invasive procedure, or permanent harm results
6	Contributed to fatal outcome

Source: Published in Hartwig SC, Denger SD, Schneider PJ: Severity indexed medication error reporting program. *Am J Hosp Pharm* 48(12):2611–2616, 1991. Used with permission of The Ohio State University, Columbus.

mance. For example, developing a pilot satellite pharmacy to prepare first doses of intravenous antibiotics could be tested to determine whether the time between a treatment decision and administration of the first dose decreased.

- *Cycle for learning: What changes can we make that will result in an improvement?* Different change concepts that could improve performance are identified and systematically tested using the measurement system and data collection to see whether improvement results and the aim is achieved. A plan-do-study-act (PDSA) cycle is used to test change concepts. All improvements require change, but not all changes result in an improvement. Using the previous example, other change concepts that might reduce the time required to initiate antibiotic therapy, in addition to a satellite pharmacy, would be the use of premade doses, faxing orders to the pharmacy, or having pharmacists participate on rounds. The goal is to develop and test change concepts on a small scale and expand the use of the changes that improve performance.

An example of an *external benchmark* is the medication error rate as determined by observation-based studies. These studies have shown the incidence of medication errors in hospitals to be as high as 15% or more in facilities with medications stocked in patient care areas.[12,13] Unit-dose programs have been shown to reduce the incidence of medication errors by approximately 50% (to about 5%).[12,13] The lowest rates of medication errors published are less than 1% and were reported at an organization with a pharmacy-coordinated unit-dose and drug administration program where consistent procedures were employed throughout the organization.[14] Recent studies have shown the incidence of medication errors to be higher in hospitals with automated medication distribution devices that bypass the review by a pharmacist.[15] This should not be surprising because these machines are only automated versions of floor stock systems that were associated with a high incidence of medication errors in the 1960s. A periodic (annual) observation-based study could be used to benchmark the performance of a similar type of organization's medication use processes against these published studies. Even if external benchmarks for performance cannot be found easily, it is important for organizations to develop institutional aims, monitor their own performance over time, and evaluate the impact of changes on performance.

Table 2-2. Medication Error Index for Categorizing Errors: National Coordinating Council for Medication Error Reporting and Prevention

Type of Error/Category	Result
No Error	
Category A	Circumstances or events that have the capacity to cause error
*Error, No Harm**	
Category B	An error occurred but the medication did not reach the patient
Category C	An error occurred that reached the patient but did not cause patient harm
Category D	An error occurred that resulted in the need for increased patient monitoring but no patient harm
Error, Harm	
Category E	An error occurred that resulted in the need for treatment or intervention and caused temporary patient harm
Category F	An error occurred that resulted in initial or prolonged hospitalization and caused temporary patient harm
Category G	An error occurred that resulted in permanent patient harm
Category H	An error occurred that resulted in a near-death event (eg, anaphylaxis, cardiac arrest)
Error, Death	
Category I	An error occurred that resulted in patient death

* The Council's definition of "harm" is "death, or temporary or permanent impairment of body function/structure requiring intervention." Intervention may include monitoring the patient's condition, change in therapy, or active medical or surgical treatment.

Source: National Coordinating Council for Medication Error Reporting and Prevention. Rockville, MD. Used with permission.

Monitoring the Performance of Medication Use Processes

The monitoring methods described in this section can be used to systematically measure the performance of each step in a medication use process. Although the discussion focuses on individual processes, it is important to keep in mind that the broader emphasis is to improve medication use throughout the organization by designing systems that will reduce the potential for error to occur.

Prescribing

Most errors in prescribing can be effectively captured through a program in which pharmacists and nurses document when they intervene with a prescriber on behalf of the patient. Nurses and pharmacists are accustomed to documenting their interventions from a medicolegal standpoint, and the information can be useful for improving the prescribing process. Once the patient care problem is resolved, the data are entered into a relational database that tracks critical data elements, such as the type of error, the potential severity or significance if the order was carried out, and the medication involved. Table 2-3 (page 30) provides an example of a severity scale for potential errors with definitions adapted from the work of Folli et al[16] and Lazar et al.[17]

Some commercially available pharmacy computer systems allow documentation of interventions during the order entry process. Pharmacy computer systems with online intervention documentation eliminate the extra step of entering

Table 2-3. Severity Definitions

Potentially Fatal or Severe

1. The ordered dose was greater than 10 times the normal dose for a medication with a low therapeutic index, and/or the serum level resulting from such a dose is likely to be in the severe toxicity range.
2. The dose of the medication ordered has a high potential to cause a life threatening adverse reaction, such as anaphylaxis or respiratory arrest from a medication allergy, or cardiopulmonary arrest.
3. The dose of a drug ordered to treat a serious illness or a potentially lifesaving drug is in a dose too low for the patient being treated.

Potentially Serious

1. The drug ordered could exacerbate the patient's condition, such as a drug–drug interaction, or drug–disease interaction.
2. Duplicate therapy with potentially serious toxic reactions was prescribed.
3. The dose ordered for medication with a low therapeutic index was 4 to 10 times the normal dose, and/or could result in serum concentrations in the toxic range.
4. The dose ordered for treatment of a serious illness was too low for the patient.
5. The wrong medication was ordered with potentially serious toxic reactions or inadequate therapy of serious illness.
6. The order was written illegibly or in a manner that could result in an error that could produce a serious toxic reaction or inadequate therapy for serious illness.

Potentially Significant

1. The dose ordered for a medication with a low therapeutic index was 1.5 to 4 times the normal dose, with a potential toxic reaction because of the dose.
2. The dose of any medication was 5 or more times greater than normal, with potential for adverse effects because of the dose.
3. The dose ordered was inadequate to produce therapeutic effects.
4. The wrong route was ordered and has the potential to produce increased adverse effects or inadequate therapy.
5. Wrong medication ordered for a nonsevere illness and there was a potential for side effects from the drug.
6. Duplicate therapy was prescribed with a potential for additive toxicity.
7. A medication order was written illegibly or in such a manner as to result in an error producing adverse effects or inadequate therapy.
8. The wrong laboratory studies are ordered to monitor a specific side effect.

Problem Orders

1. Duplicate therapy was ordered without potential for increased adverse effects.
2. The order was missing information necessary to complete it (drug, dose, dosage strength, formulation, route, or frequency).
3. The wrong route was ordered without potential for adverse reactions or therapeutic failure.
4. The dose ordered was 5 times greater than normal but without toxic potential.
5. An errant order was written that was unlikely to be carried out.

Revised 6/30/93

Source: The Ohio State University Medical Center, Columbus. Used with permission.

data into a separate database and can provide an efficient way to capture necessary information. In the absence of such a system, a manual data collection form can be developed. Trending the data can clearly show the performance of the prescribing process. For example, an error in prescribing a medication to which a patient is allergic has the potential for serious consequences if not intercepted. If a trend in such errors is identified, actions can be taken to prevent these errors from occurring through prescriber education or modification of procedures.

Over time, the effectiveness of actions taken also can be assessed. Prescriber errors intercepted by either nurses or pharmacists are important in improving the prescribing process because they provide the opportunity to make changes before any harm has occurred. A performance measure using this type of data is the number of pharmacist and nurse interventions stratified by severity or type of drug with the denominator of total orders written by prescribers. This measure can provide information to help focus more detailed studies. It also provides a more accurate reflection of the effectiveness of improvement efforts because the numbers are adjusted for specific activities. For example, the number of ampicillin-sulbactam orders written for penicillin-allergic patients that are corrected, divided by the total number of orders for ampicillin-sulbactam in a defined time period would measure one element of prescribing performance.

Prescribing errors that are not detected and corrected and result in adverse drug events can be captured through a voluntary reporting system or by surveillance systems. Computerized systems that screen for abnormal laboratory values, abnormal clinical data, use of antidote medications, and medication stop orders are examples of such surveillance systems.[18,19] These events can be used to trigger a medical record review that may identify a prescribing error as a contributing factor to an adverse drug event. For example, a computerized

screen for injectable vitamin K (phytonadione) orders could be used to identify patients who are potentially over-anticoagulated. A medical record review of these cases could be compared to acceptable clinical practice to determine whether there is an opportunity to improve the use of anticoagulants in the facility or a group of patients. Trends identified through these surveillance systems can be used to formulate action plans to affect change and improve prescribing practices. An example of a system that could be developed is the review of all preventable adverse drug events captured by incident reports and surveillance techniques.

A well-established method for evaluating the prescribing process is the use of criteria-based audits or medication use evaluation studies. It is important that physicians, nurses, and pharmacists be involved in defining the criteria that will be used to assess the prescribing process. The criteria must be compared to accepted clinical practice through a review of the literature and guidelines in similar organizations. The priorities for evaluation are best decided by multidisciplinary consensus after review of organization-specific information. This information can be obtained by trending data from incident reports, intervention reports, and computer surveillance reports. The criteria usually focus on a narrow topic that has been identified as problem prone or high risk through ongoing data review. If, for example, there were reports of acute gastrointestinal bleeding in patients receiving ketorolac, it might be useful to perform an audit on the prescribing of ketorolac based on age, weight, and renal function. Such an audit would provide information on how often the medication was prescribed inappropriately and by whom. The information obtained from the audit could be used as objective evidence to support recommendations for prescriber education, guideline development, and policy modifications such as automatic substitution of appropriate doses by clinical pharmacists. It is worth emphasizing that education should be included in the action plan regardless of what other methods are chosen to improve the process.

Monitoring prescribing during interdisciplinary patient care rounds is an observation-based program in which pharmacists, nurses, and physicians review prescribing decisions when they are made. Errors are prevented before medication orders are written. This method is especially useful in teaching hospitals. It is also expensive and may be limited to practice settings where high-risk, problem-prone drug therapy is prescribed, as in an intensive care unit.

Transcribing

Errors in transcription can be linked to multiple processes in the medication use system. In many cases, determining that the cause of a medication error as a missed or incorrect transcription is relatively straightforward, although it may be elusive if the person checking also misreads the order. An illegible or poorly written order reflects a performance deficit in the prescribing process. An error in transcribing the prescription order to a dispensing record, whether computerized or manual, represents a failure in the dispensing process. A missed or incomplete transcription of a medication order to an administration record can reflect mistakes in medication administration and monitoring. Identifying mistakes in transcription as a cause of medication errors enables an organization to focus on procedures used to transcribe medication orders. In a voluntary reporting system, failures in transcription can be captured by requesting the reporter to identify the cause of the error. Because it is usually not practical to personally follow up on each report filed, it is desirable to design the incident report so the question of why the error occurred will be answered when the

initial report is submitted. The trending of medication error data obtained from incident reports is much more efficient if error types and causes are predefined, standardized terms printed on the report form.

Criteria-based audits are another method of measurement useful in evaluating transcription errors. They can consist of comparing physician orders, pharmacy dispensing records, and medication administration records for inconsistencies. The primary focus of such audits is most often medication administration; however, errors in transcribing are sometimes identified as the cause of administration errors. The audits are usually conducted by pharmacists and nurses. Baseline data are obtained before a process or procedure change is instituted, and the audit is repeated after a certain period of time to assess the effects of the change.

Dispensing

Medication errors resulting from mistakes in dispensing can be captured through a voluntary reporting program. If the error is not detected and intercepted by the existing inspection system—usually a check by the nurse or patient—and the medication reaches the patient and causes harm, it is categorized as a *preventable adverse drug event*. The data can be tracked in a relational database as described earlier. Dispensing errors are often related to process faults, and voluntary error reports can help identify trends so they can be corrected.

Traditionally, the dispensing function has been associated with the pharmacist. However, it is important to recognize that there may be times when nurses and physicians are responsible for dispensing. Point-of-care automated dispensing systems and floor stock systems are examples of how nurses perform the dispensing function. Another example of nonpharmacist dispensing consists of in-house pharmacies that do not provide 24-hour service and have provisions or policies for nurse access to medications after hours. Physicians may dispense in clinics, in special procedure areas, in operating rooms, during emergent situations, and under similar circumstances. In these situations, the established safety nets for ensuring that the patient receives the correct medication (that is, physician prescribing, pharmacist dispensing, and nurse administering) is bypassed, thereby increasing the chance of errors.

System bypass errors identified through reporting programs may alert the organization that alternate systems for medication dispensing lack the fundamental safeguards necessary for error prevention. A hypothetical example of such an error is a decimal place prescribing error for 2.5 mg of digoxin IV (usual dose is 0.25 mg) that is carried out by a nurse who, to prepare the dose, obtains 10 digoxin syringes out of an automated dispensing machine and administers the dose. As a result of a lack of prior experience, he or she may not have considered this an unusual dose. In the traditional system of responsibilities, there would be a higher likelihood that this wrong-dose error would have been detected and corrected before reaching the patient. Such an error would be serious and trigger a root cause analysis that might suggest, among other actions, a need for pharmacist review of orders before certain medications can be obtained from automated dispensing systems. Another effective action would be to reduce the amount of digoxin available at any one time to an amount that could not cause harm even if administered in error. Removing digoxin injection from automated dispensing systems completely is another alternative, but it is important to balance the benefit of having a medication readily available in an emergency situation against the risk of bypassing the traditional check and balance system. Individuals who are involved in making decisions about dispensing systems need to be familiar with all facets of the organization's existing system.

Meaningful monitors of the dispensing process include order turnaround time (sometimes reflected in the number of late or omitted doses), cart filling errors, floor stock or automated dispensing machine stocking errors, and transcription errors in dispensing records. These data can be captured through voluntary reporting or criteria-based audits. Errors in product selection from automated dispensing machines may suggest the need to change the placement of medication to minimize the potential for mix-ups with similar sounding names or look-alike packaging. It would be dangerous to place injectable hydroxyzine and hydralazine next to each other or even in the same matrix drawer. This sounds like a relatively simple concept, but maintenance requires ongoing vigilance, especially in organizations whose buying groups often change products and manufacturers.

Documentation and tracking of dispensing errors made during the filling of unit-dose patient medication bins in the pharmacy is an observation-based system. These data can be used to provide constructive feedback to the individuals who fill and check carts by graphing performance over time and displaying the graph where medication bins are filled. The effects of actions such as education, changes in procedures, minimization of interruptions, and optimization of environment on the frequency of cart filling errors can be assessed. An ideal way to present such data is by showing the percentage of medication carts filled correctly each week or month on a bar graph (with an established goal of 100%), thereby emphasizing accuracy as opposed to errors.

Administering

Medication administration errors have been the traditional focus of incident reporting programs. As discussed in previous sections, administration errors are frequently the events that identify a failure in other processes. A wrong medication may be administered because it was prescribed, transcribed, or dispensed incorrectly. Errors in administration that do not have an apparent underlying cause, such as incorrect use of equipment, wrong transcription, and so on, are usually described as "human errors" resulting from a performance deficit. The person administering the medication simply failed to verify the dose, drug, time, route, or patient name. In most cases, an underlying cause *can* be identified. Factors such as patient load or practitioner fatigue or acuity may contribute to these types of errors. As described in the earlier section on identifying and measuring prescribing errors, the trending of the cause of the error tends to provide the most useful information in designing strategies for future error prevention. An example of an underlying cause of wrong-dose errors may be improper use of infusion equipment, such as failure to accurately program a pump or mishandling of infusion tubing which can result in free flow of intravenous medication. An action plan to correct these underlying causes may include education of staff and acquisition of technology that protects against free flow of intravenous infusions.

Medication administration errors can be detected through observation. Observation-based studies are useful in periodically assessing an organization's true medication error rate and in identifying the frequency of each type of drug administration error, including wrong drug, omission, wrong route, wrong dose, and wrong time. Observation-based studies also may be used to validate error types reported through voluntary reporting programs. If omission errors are the most common errors found through voluntary reporting and are identified as the most common error type in an observation-based study, an organization may cautiously conclude that medication administration errors reported voluntarily are representative of true errors.

Criteria-based audits of medication administration have been used by nursing departments to evaluate the medication administration record for complete and accurate documentation. The method can be useful in measuring the medication error rate. An audit may be designed to compare physician orders to medication administration records and document discrepancies. Evaluations can determine whether medications were administered as ordered or scheduled. When medications are not administered as ordered, the reviewer can judge whether the event was an administration error. Most medication administration documentation procedures require that the reason for an omitted dose be documented on the record. If no such documentation is provided, the reviewer assumes a medication error occurred. Underlying causes, such as missed/incorrect transcription of orders or delays in order processing or medication delivery, are often identified. The error rate can be calculated by dividing the number of errors by the number of doses scheduled to be administered (that is, the number of opportunities for error). An example of a medication administration audit form is shown in Figure 2-3 (page 35). Such an audit can be used to monitor and assess all medication use processes.

Monitoring of Medication Effects

Review of information about adverse drug events represents the most commonly used method for assessing the monitoring component of medication use. Preventable adverse drug events are usually identified through voluntary reporting and by screening of clinical laboratory and pharmacy data. Voluntary reporting of adverse drug events is frequently done through incident reporting programs, telephone reporting, and online documentation of adverse drug events not linked to incident reports. Record review can help to determine whether an adverse drug event

Medication Administration Audit Form

Tampa General Healthcare
Department of Pharmaceutical Care
Medication Administration Record Audit

Patient Care Unit: _____   MR #: _____   Date: _____   By: _____

Medication Transcription Audit	Total # Orders Reviewed	YES	NO	% Compliance	Comments: medications involved, did an ADE occur, did error reach patient, significance/severity
		RPh	RN		
Compare Rx Profile to MAR to Physician Orders					
Correct medication transcription					
Complete medication transcription					
No discontinued orders are active					
No duplicate medication entries					
PRN orders are qualified					

Medications Administration Audit (circle or indicate next to # if 0 or 1)	All Meds	IV Admixture	Critical Meds*	Comments: medications involved, did an ADE occur, did error reach patient, significance/severity
Total # of doses scheduled to be administered				
Total # of doses charted as administered				
Total # of doses given on time (within 1 hour window)				
# scheduled changes due to omitted/late medications				
# omitted/late because not available				
# omitted/late with appropriate documentation (refused, procedure)				
# omitted/late with incomplete documentation				

*Critical medications: antibiotics, pain medications, antihypertensive medications

Prescribing/Monitoring Audit	Total # Orders Reviewed	YES	NO	% Compliance	Comments
Doses adjusted for age/organ function					
No meds ordered to which patient is allergic†					
Orders are complete					
PRN orders are qualified					
No therapeutic duplication					

†Do not include cross sensitivities like cephalosporins and penicillins—only true allergies

Audit time frame = 24 hours

Figure 2-3. *All medication use processes, including medication administration, can be assessed using this form. ADE, adverse drug event; IV, intravenous; MAR, medication administration record; MR, medical record; PRN, pro re na'ta (as needed); RN, registered nurse; RPh, registered pharmacist; Rx, prescription.*

Source: Tampa General Healthcare, Florida. Used with permission.

occurred and to characterize the nature of the event, the underlying cause, and any change in patient outcome. If a preventable adverse drug event is confirmed, the data are then included in the database that tracks medication errors and adverse drug events.

With today's computer technology, it is possible to design a sophisticated method for screening and identifying adverse drug events. An example of such a system is that developed by the Intermountain Healthcare Corporation.[19, 20] The system is designed to perform computerized surveillance of adverse drug events in hospitalized patients. An important feature of the system is the automated detection of flags that identify potential adverse drug events. These signals include abnormal laboratory values, orders for antidote medications, and numerous other identifiers. Less sophisticated but effective methods are used by most clinical pharmacists to identify, prevent, and resolve adverse events in their daily practice. Automating the process simply makes it more efficient in identifying and tracking adverse drug events.

Errors in monitoring may include the failure to act on laboratory and other diagnostic tests and the failure to assess the achievement of a therapeutic endpoint, such as a cure for disease or control of symptoms. This type of data lends itself to evaluation by the use of criteria. For example, an audit to measure the rate at which empiric antibiotic therapy is converted to definitive therapy when culture and sensitivity data become available might provide significant opportunities to improve the way patients are monitored. In addition to the monitoring process, this type of audit would evaluate the prescribing process and have the potential to involve several clinical departments, such as laboratory and microbiology or epidemiology.

Improving the Medication Use System

Medication use affects virtually all patients across the continuum of care, making improving medication use processes an important activity in any health care organization. Measuring, managing, and improving the medication use system is part of a broad strategy and administrative focus on quality improvement. For each of the processes involved, performance measurement methods are developed, performance standards are set, and the process is improved to meet or exceed the standards. Quality improvement of all medication use processes affects activities in all areas of a health care organization, including pharmacy and therapeutics committee activities, infection control activities, development and revision of patient care policies and practice guidelines, clinical quality management activities, risk management, care coordination and case management, implementation of information systems, and patient satisfaction activities.

Improving the medication use process is a broad-based initiative that requires a pervasive involvement in all forums and venues where patient care is discussed and delivered. It is nearly impossible to evaluate one component of the medication use process at a time because the performance of the processes is interdependent. The intent of this chapter was not to compartmentalize the processes but to assist the reader in developing meaningful measurements that will assess the ability of his or her existing medication use system to prevent errors and to evaluate the effectiveness of improvement strategies.

Medication errors have been discussed throughout this and the previous chapter as indicators to be measured and monitored. Chapter 3 explains what a medication error is and gives examples of the different types of errors that may present opportunities for improvement.

References

1. Churchill GA: *Marketing Research Methodological Foundations,* 6th ed. Fort Worth, TX: The Dryden Press, 1995, pp 636–639.

2. Kirk RE: *Experimental Design: Procedures for the Behavioral Sciences,* 2nd ed. Pacific Grove, CA: Brooks and Cole, 1982, pp 308–349.

3. Allan EL, Barker KN: Fundamentals of medication error research. *Am J Hosp Pharm* 47:555–571, 1990.

4. Ryan KD, Oestreich DK: *Driving Fear Out of the Workplace.* San Francisco: Jossey-Bass, 1991.

5. Ryan KD, Oestreich DK, Orr GA: *The Courageous Messenger.* San Francisco: Jossey-Bass, 1997.

6. Nadzam DM: Development of medication-use indicators by the Joint Commission on Accreditation of Healthcare Organizations. *Am J Hosp Pharm* 48:1925–1930, 1991.

7. ASHP guidelines on medication-use evaluation. *Am J Health Syst Pharm* 53:1953–1955, 1996.

8. Hartwig SC, Denger SD, Schneider PJ: Severity indexed medication error reporting program. *Am J Hosp Pharm* 48:2611–2616, 1991.

9. Schneider PJ, Hartwig SC: Use of severity indexed medication error reports to improve quality. *Hosp Pharm* 29:205–215, 1994.

10. Hartwig SC, Siegel J, Schneider PJ: Preventability and severity assessment in reporting adverse drug reactions. *Am J Hosp Pharm* 49:2229–2232, 1992.

11. Langley GJ, et al: *The Improvement Guide.* San Francisco: Jossey-Bass, 1996.

12. Hynniman CE, Conrad WF, Urch WA, et al: A comparison of medication errors under the University of Kentucky unit dose system and traditional drug distribution systems in four hospitals. *Am J Hosp Pharm* 27:802–814, 1970.

13. Means BJ, Derewicz HJ, Lamy PP: Medication errors in a multidose and computer based unit dose drug distribution system. *Am J Hosp Pharm* 32:186–191, 1975.

14. Shultz SM, White SJ, Latiolais CJ: Medication errors reduced by unit dose. *Hospitals* 47(6):106–112, 1973.

15. Barker KN, et al: Effect of an automated bedside dispensing machine in medication errors. *Am J Hosp Pharm* 41:1352–1358, 1984.

16. Folli HL, et al: Medication error prevention by clinical pharmacists in two children's hospitals. *Pediatrics* 79:718–722, 1987.

17. Lesar TS, et al: Medication prescribing errors in a teaching hospital. *JAMA* 263:2329–2334, 1991.

18. Classen DC, et al: Computerized surveillance of adverse drug events in hospital patients. *JAMA* 266:2847–2851, 1991.

19. Classen DC, et al: Description of a computerized adverse drug event monitor using a hospital information system. *Hosp Pharm* 27:74,776–779,783, 1992.

Chapter 3

DEFINING MEDICATION ERRORS

Diane DeMichele Cousins, RPh
Vice President, Practitioner Reporting Programs
United States Pharmacopeia
Rockville, Maryland

In the continuum of care, medication use is just one facet of the complex health care system. Medication use begins with prescribing and encompasses each successive process through preparation, administration or use, and monitoring. Medication errors may occur in each phase and represent one of the prevalent indicators for improvement of the system. For a health care organization to use the measurement and monitoring techniques described in Chapter 2 effectively, it must have an established definition of medication error. This chapter provides a nationally accepted definition and, through case reports, demonstrates how errors are classified by specific and general causes.

What Is a Medication Error?

Definitions of *medication error* have varied among clinicians, researchers, and administrators to such an extent that valid comparison for any purpose is difficult at best. For example, researchers have calculated medication error rates including or excluding wrong-time errors and omission errors. Some reporting systems may count only those errors that are intercepted or those that reach the patient.

Broadly defined, medication errors are "episodes in drug misadventuring that should be preventable through effective systems controls."[1] By contrast, early medication errors research generally defined an *error* as "a deviation from the physician's medication order as written on the patient's chart."[2,3] Considering the medication use system as a whole, errors can obviously occur during any of the core processes. The calculation of error rates should therefore use the sum of all the doses ordered plus all the unordered doses given (that is, total opportunities for error)[2] as a denominator. Likewise, the "physician's order" should be termed the "prescriber's order" to reflect the growing number of categories of health care professionals with prescriptive authority.

Physicians, nurses, and pharmacists have long been seen as the sole human causes of medication errors. Only in recent years have the broad multidisciplinary aspects of medication errors become recognized. In fact, medication errors may be committed by both experienced and inexperienced health professionals, supportive personnel (for example, pharmacy technicians), students, clerical staff (for example, ward clerks), administrators, and even patients and their caregivers.[1] No individual performing part of the medication use function is immune to error.

In July 1995, the National Coordinating Council for Medication Error Reporting and Prevention, representing the collaboration of some of the nation's leading health care and consumer organizations, convened to begin addressing the growing concerns related to medication errors. As a first step the Council established this definition:

> A medication error is any preventable event that may cause or lead to inappropriate medication use or patient harm while the medication is in the control of the health care professional, patient, or consumer. Such events may be related to professional practice, health care products, procedures, and systems, including prescribing; order communication; product labeling, packaging, and nomenclature; compounding; dispensing; distribution; administration; education; monitoring; and use.[4]

This definition includes potential errors, that is, circumstances or events with the capacity to cause error,[4] and actual errors; errors that reach the patient and those that are intercepted; and those errors by health care professionals and by consumers and caregivers. The Council encourages the use of this definition by researchers, who can provide a consistent framework that standardizes error classification and analysis, and by facilities, that can integrate this definition into the design of in-house reporting mechanisms. This standardized definition should establish the initial basis for national benchmarking.

Classification of Errors

Medication error types have been categorized in a variety of ways, but the most useful to date was developed by the American Society of Health-System Pharmacists (ASHP) in its "Guidelines on Preventing Medication Errors in Hospitals."[1] Each type is defined in Table 3-1 (page 41), and inclusions and exclusions are identified. When applying this classification to medication error reports, the 12 types of errors may not be mutually exclusive

because of the inherent complexity of most errors in any given process; therefore, the categories will not be additive when calculating overall error rates.

At this writing, the National Coordinating Council for Medication Error Reporting and Prevention is preparing a taxonomy of error which will include not only a similar listing of types of errors but also classify errors according to their cause, the setting in which they occur, therapeutic classification of drugs involved, and patient outcome. The Council intends for this taxonomy to become a standardized tool for organizing and coding error information.

Applying Standardized Error Classifications to Real-World Cases

Capturing errors and classifying them by type is the first step in problem definition and system analysis. Allan and Barker stress the importance of using operational definitions to promote reliability and allow comparison with other data.[3] The standardized definition of medication error given earlier and the ASHP's list of types of errors provide the cornerstones for any health care organization's medication error reporting program and serve as important steps toward national benchmarking.

Benchmarking at the national level cannot take place without data, and the U.S. Pharmacopeia (USP) Medication Errors Reporting (MER) Program* is compiling such data. In August 1991, the USP assumed responsibility for coordinating

---

*The USP (U.S. Pharmacopeia) is a private, not-for-profit organization that sets legally enforceable standards for drug products. The USP MER Program is presented in cooperation with the Institute for Safe Medication Practices and is a partner in the U.S. Food and Drug Administration (FDA) MedWatch Program. Because of the range of people and organizations that may be affected by medication errors, the USP also shares its reports with product manufacturers, the FDA, the Institute for Safe Medication Practices, the U.S. Adopted Names Council (USAN), and the National Coordinating Council for Medication Error Reporting and Prevention.

Table 3-1. Types of Medication Errors*

Prescribing error	Incorrect drug selection (based on indications, contraindications, known allergies, existing drug therapy, and other factors), dose, dosage form, quantity, route, concentration, rate of administration, or instructions for use of a drug product ordered or authorized by physician (or other legitimate prescriber); illegible prescriptions or medication orders that lead to errors that reach the patient
Omission error[†]	The failure to administer an ordered dose to a patient before the next scheduled dose, if any
Wrong time error	Administration of medication outside a predefined time interval from its scheduled administration time (this interval should be established by each individual health care facility)
Unauthorized drug error[‡]	Administration to the patient of medication not authorized by a legitimate prescriber for the patient
Improper dose error[§]	Administration to the patient of a dose that is greater than or less than the amount ordered by the prescriber or administration of duplicate doses to the patient, for example, one or more dosage units in addition to those that were ordered
Wrong dosage–form error[¶]	Administration to the patient of a drug product in a different dosage form than ordered by the prescriber
Wrong drug-preparation error[#]	Drug product incorrectly formulated or manipulated before administration
Wrong administration–technique error**	Inappropriate procedure or improper technique in the administration of a drug
Deteriorated drug error[††]	Administration of a drug that has expired or for which the physical or chemical dosage-form integrity has been compromised
Monitoring error	Failure to review a prescribed regimen for appropriateness and detection of problems, or failure to use appropriate clinical or laboratory data for adequate assessment of patient response to prescribed therapy
Compliance error	Inappropriate patient behavior regarding adherence to a prescribed medication regimen
Other medication error	Any medication error that does not fall into one of the above predefined categories

* The categories may not be mutually exclusive because of the multidisciplinary and multifactorial nature of medication errors.

[†] Assumes no prescribing error. Excluded would be (1) a patient's refusal to take the medication or (2) a decision not to administer the dose because of recognized contraindications. If an explanation for the omission is apparent (for example, patient was away from nursing unit for tests or medication was not available), that reason should be documented in the appropriate records.

[‡] This would include, for example, a wrong drug, a dose given to the wrong patient, unordered drugs, and doses given outside a stated set of clinical guidelines or protocols.

[§] Excluded would be (1) allowable deviations based on preset ranges established by individual health care organizations in consideration of measuring devices routinely provided to those who administer drugs to patients (for example, not administering a dose based on patient's measured temperature or blood glucose level) or other factors such as conversion of doses expressed in the apothecary system to the metric system and (2) topical dosage forms for which medication orders are not expressed quantitatively.

[¶] Excluded would be accepted protocols (established by the pharmacy and therapeutics committee or its equivalent) that authorize pharmacists to dispense alternate dosage forms for patients with special needs (for example, liquid formulations for patients with nasogastric tubes or those who have difficulty swallowing), as allowed by state regulations.

[#] This would include, for example, incorrect dilution or reconstitution, mixing drugs that are physically or chemically incompatible, and inadequate product packaging.

** This would include doses administered (1) via the wrong route (different from the route prescribed), (2) via the correct route but at the wrong site (for example, left eye instead of right), and (3) at the wrong rate of administration.

[††] This would include, for example, administration of expired drugs and improperly stored drugs.

Source: Originally published in *American Journal of Hospital Pharmacy* 50(2):306, 1993. ©1993 American Society of Hospital Pharmacists, Inc. All rights reserved. Reprinted with permission (R9852).

the Medication Errors Reporting Program initially developed by the Institute for Safe Medication Practices. The USP MER Program captures a wide range of errors, including potential errors, interventions, and prescribing errors.[5] Its threefold purpose is to

- heighten national awareness of medication errors;
- develop educational programs and materials; and
- effect changes in *United States Pharmacopeia-National Formulary* (*USP-NF*) standards and drug information in the USP Drug Information (USP DI) database.

Reports to the USP MER Program are voluntary and may be submitted anonymously (Figure 3-1, page 43). The program database comprises 22 fields of information about actual and potential errors, including the setting in which the error occurred, the type of intervention that prevented the error from reaching the patient, reporter recommendations for avoiding future errors, and the level of staff involved in the error. Errors are classified by severity, type, and cause.

The case reports presented in this section represent incidents as described in program reports. They provide illustrative examples of many of the types of medication errors identified in Table 3-1. Whereas the ASHP definitions of types of errors are not operationally specific,[3] the cases help to explain the definitions. Each case description is followed by a discussion, including the reporter's recommendation for preventing a recurrence of the error and any policies or procedures instituted by the reporter. In reviewing the cases, the reader is encouraged to consider the systems or process changes that could help prevent similar errors in his or her own organization.

Prescribing Error

Case Report 040085. A physician wrote an order for Dilaudid® (hydromorphone) 50 mg intramus-

cularly (IM) instead of Demerol® (meperidine) 50 mg IM for a 55-year-old female patient, who was one day post-lumbar laminectomy. The nurse called the physician and questioned the order, but was told to give the medication. The nurse had to call several pharmacies in the hospital to gather the amount needed for this massive dose. The medication was given and the patient went into respiratory arrest, followed by cerebral anoxia, and eventual incapacitation. She was discharged in a chronic vegetative state on the post-event day 70.

Discussion. This case illustrates the psychosocial authority barriers that must be broken down in order to approach errors in a systematic way. The role of the nurse (and the pharmacist) must be bolstered to act as a systems check to catch possible prescribing errors. The environment must be conducive to open discussion without intimidation, denigration, or punishment. Until an organization's culture reaches a desired level of openness in its communication, a method needs to be established to resolve such conflicts, to provide recourse, and to protect the patient. Also, using multiple vials (especially more than two) to prepare a single dose should serve as an immediate flag to recheck a medication order. Computerized dose-range checks would have been useful in this case for immediately alerting the physician to an error.

Omission Error

Case Report 041998. On day 1, a patient's preoperative orders were written, stating that nothing should be given by mouth (NPO) after midnight. The admitting diagnosis for this patient, a 77-year-old Type 1 diabetic with end-stage renal disease, was surgical drainage of a septic shoulder. On day 2, the surgery was postponed until the following day, but the patient's morning insulin dose was held anyway. In fact, he received no food until his renal diet dinner and later, 20 units of insulin was administered. That evening, the

USP Medication Errors Reporting Form

USP MEDICATION ERRORS REPORTING PROGRAM
Presented in cooperation with the Institute for Safe Medication Practices
The USP Practitioners' Reporting Network℠ is an FDA MEDWATCH partner

MEDICATION ERRORS REPORTING PROGRAM

❏ ACTUAL ERROR   ❏ POTENTIAL ERROR

Please describe the error. Include sequence of events, personnel involved, and work environment (e.g., code situation, change of shift, short staffing, no 24-hr. pharmacy, floor stock). If more space is needed, please attach separate page.

Was the medication administered to or used by the patient? ❏ No ❏ Yes   Date and time of event: _____

What type of staff or health care practitioner made the initial error? _____

Describe outcome (e.g., death, type of injury, adverse reaction). _____

If the medication did not reach the patient, describe the intervention. _____

Who discovered the error? _____

When and how was error discovered? _____

Where did the error occur (e.g., hospital, outpatient or retail pharmacy, nursing home, patient's home)? _____

Was another practitioner involved in the error ? ❏ No ❏ Yes If yes, what type of practitioner? _____

Was patient counseling provided? ❏ No ❏ Yes If yes, before or after error was discovered? _____

If a product was involved, please complete the following:

	Product #1	Product #2
Brand name of product involved		
Generic name		
Manufacturer		
Labeler (if different from mfr.)		
Dosage form		
Strength/concentration		
Type and size of container		
NDC number		

If available, please provide relevant patient information (age, gender, diagnosis, etc.). Patient identification not required.

Reports are most useful when relevant materials such as product label, copy of prescription/order, etc. can be reviewed. Can these materials be provided? ❏ No ❏ Yes If yes, please specify. _____

Suggest any recommendations you have to prevent recurrence of this error or describe policies or procedures you have instituted to prevent future similar errors.

A copy of this report is routinely sent to the Institute for Safe Medication Practices (ISMP), to the manufacturer/labeler, and to the Food and Drug Administration (FDA). **USP may release my identity to: (check boxes that apply)**

❏ ISMP ❏ The manufacturer and/or labeler as listed above ❏ FDA ❏ Other persons requesting a copy of this report ❏ Anonymous to all

Your name and title _____

Your facility name, address, and ZIP _____

Telephone number (include area code) _____

Signature _____   Date _____

Return to the attention of:
Diane D. Cousins, R.Ph.
USP PRN
12601 Twinbrook Parkway
Rockville, MD 20852-1790

Call Toll Free: 800-23-ERROR (800-233-7767)
or FAX 301-816-8532
USP home page: http://www.usp.org
Electronic reporting forms are available. Please call for
additional information and/or your free diskette.

Date Received by USP: _____   File Access Number: _____

C-194

Additional forms can be found in the *USP DI Vol. I* and *Vol. III* and in all monthly *Updates*.

Figure 3-1. *This form is used by participants in the USP Medication Errors Reporting Program to submit errors for inclusion in the program database. Reports are voluntary.*

Source: USP Medication Errors Reporting Program, Rockville, MD. Used with permission.

surgery was once again rescheduled (for day 4). The patient received no other food on day 2, and glucose supplements were not given on days 1 or 2. On day 3, the patient was found unresponsive and hypoglycemic (<20 mg/dL). The unconscious patient arrested, regained normal sinus rhythm after resuscitation, but later expired after withdrawal of life support.

Discussion. This dose omission error was not detected through several nursing shift changes but should have been. The hospital conducted an inservice for intensive care unit (ICU) staff on the management of NPO surgical diabetic patients. Organizations should have a diabetic/insulin protocol to help prevent such errors. Creating a diabetes nurse position to monitor these patients is also helpful.

Wrong-Time Error
Case Report 04211. When the hospital pharmacy began receiving medication orders for lispro insulin, the pharmacist discovered that nursing staff was administering a supply of nonformulary lispro to two patients 30 minutes prior to meals (per inpatient nursing policy for other insulins). Unlike other insulins, lispro should be administered no more than 15 minutes before the meal.

Discussion. As with many errors, this situation is multifaceted. Because the endocrinologist could not obtain insulin lispro injection immediately when filling out a formulary request form, he obtained samples from the manufacturer's representative. (This begs for an organizationwide policy to control drugs supplied by company representatives, centralize control of pharmaceuticals, and limit floor stock items.) Nursing staff was unfamiliar with this new, rapid-acting product but appropriate training was not initiated. The hospital instituted some excellent error prevention strategies in the interim:

- The product *must* be ordered as "lispro."
- Lime green stickers are placed on each vial with instructions to "take with meals."
- For all lispro orders, "to take with meals" is automatically printed on the medication administration record.
- Guidelines have been developed for use of lispro insulin in adult and pediatric patients.

Of course, the hospital also could have initiated a policy for nonformulary drugs if one was not in place.

Unauthorized Drug Error
Case Report 050165. An experienced pediatric oncology nurse entered the room of a six-month-old child and proceeded to give him his last dose of chemotherapy before he was discharged. His mother was present and protested that she thought he had completed his chemotherapy. The nurse persisted and proceeded to administer a 2-mg dose of vincristine to the child. The dose was intended for a 16-year-old patient on the same pediatric/adolescent ward. The syringe was properly drawn up and labeled by pharmacy. The outer bag and the barrel of the syringe had the correct patient's name affixed. The error was immediately recognized and measures were taken to prevent paralytic ileus. Although the child was transferred to a local children's hospital for further follow-up and in case invasive measures (surgery) became necessary, he suffered no adverse consequences by six months after the event.

Discussion. This case stresses the importance of paying careful attention to the concerns of patients and caregivers. It would have taken only another few moments to double-check the mother's statement, the syringe label, and the patient's identity. If this facility had been fully automated, identification of the patient and the dose through bar-codes immediately would have detected the error.

Improper Dose

Case Report 042256. A postpartum patient, who was to receive a magnesium sulfate intravenous (IV) drip (100 mg/mL) at 30 mL/hour, was found unresponsive and in respiratory arrest. She coded and was transferred to the intensive care unit. The pump was found to be infusing magnesium sulfate at 310 mL/hour for approximately 15 minutes. The patient was treated and recovered. The registered nurse programming the pump had been asked to hang the IV bag as she was moving on to the next patient. She thought she had entered the total *volume* to be infused (310 mL), but actually entered 310 as the *rate* of infusion (mL/hour).

Discussion. Improper dose errors can occur with any drug. There are many reasons for improper dose errors, a few of which are

- miscalculation;

- miscommunication;

- confusion caused by differing conventions for similar product labels of different strengths of the same drug;

- similar dosage forms for different strengths of the same drug; and

- misuse of zeros, resulting in ten-fold differences in strength (leading zeros, such as 0.1 mg, should be required and trailing zeros, such as 1.0 mg, should be prohibited in prescription writing as per USP-NF recommendation).

Improper dose errors with magnesium sulfate have been caused by these and other factors. For this reason, special care should be taken in the storage and handling of this drug. The hospital involved in this magnesium sulfate error and other organizations that have experienced similar errors have made the following system process changes:

- Dosing for IV magnesium sulfate is only written in mEq (or grams) and computer order-entry supports this restriction;

- Guidelines, including infusion rates and maximum doses, were developed for IV magnesium sulfate replacement therapy;

- A conversion chart for the various expressions of magnesium sulfate strength was developed for use by physicians, pharmacists, and nurses; and

- Magnesium sulfate is only available in premixed minibags and large-volume parenterals. If magnesium sulfate *must* be stored in patient care areas, the organization should consider minimizing the volume per container that is available.

Wrong Dosage-Form Error

Case Report 050092. A pharmacist in an outpatient clinic filled a written prescription for Atrovent® Nasal Spray with Atrovent® Inhalation Aerosol (for oral use). No unusual aspects of the work environment were noted at the time of the error. Because Atrovent® Nasal Spray was not on the organization's formulary, the Atrovent® Oral Aerosol was the only dosage form available. The prescription was clearly written. At the time of patient counseling, the box was not opened in the presence of the patient, and the patient declined a demonstration.

Discussion. Stocking only a subset of the 10,000-plus drug products available still requires some knowledge of items not stocked. Sometimes staff believe that a prescription is inaccurate or incomplete if the drug name, dosage form, or strength prescribed is not exactly the same as that on the formulary. Complicated by unclear labeling or confusing packaging, a knowledge deficit about the nonformulary product can go undetected.

Wrong Drug-Preparation Error

Case Report 042166. An order was written for irinotecan 260 mg, which is packaged in a 5-mL vial containing 20 mg/*mL*. A pharmacist ordered the drug from the wholesaler, but she misread the package label as 20 mg/*vial* and ordered the purchase of several vials to deliver the dose. Fortunately, she caught the error prior to mixing the drug. A second pharmacist also misread the label as 20 mg/vial. He prepared a dose of 1,300 mg instead of the intended dose of 260 mg. The overdose was administered to the patient, who died as a result.

Discussion. In this case, it was suggested that the product be labeled with the total vial strength (100 mg/5 mL) as are other oncolytic agents. The various expressions of product strength (for example, mg/mL or mg/vial) that appear on labels require health care professionals to read the label very carefully before preparing a dose or calculating admixtures. Type sizes can be difficult to read, important information may be poorly placed, and labeling conventions may be inconsistent from product to product. It is wise to stock products that are clearly labeled.

Wrong Route of Administration Error

Case Report 050081. An 83-year-old patient died after being injected with a solution of prescription drugs that she had refused to take orally. The nurse crushed tablets of Paxil ® (paroxetine, an antidepressant), potassium chloride, and a multivitamin and combined them in sterile water. She then injected the mixture into the patient's central venous line.

Discussion. Cases of wrong administration route are not as rare as one might think, nor are they as simplistic as an intramuscular drug being administered intravenously. In fact, the USP has received numerous cases like the one described here. Although the issue is clearly one of education, there are also cer-

tain system changes that can help prevent these errors. To avoid administering injections with oral syringes, amber-colored plastic syringes and an "oral" sticker on the barrel and/or plunger can clearly identify the correct match. Where possible, tubing and oral syringes with incompatible connections should be used. A labeling policy for all patient lines—such as color coding—should be developed to help emphasize correct routes. All crushing of tablets should be cleared with the pharmacy to avoid wrong route errors and also to prevent destruction of the drug release properties of enteric and time-release dosage forms. Crushed oral tablets should *never* be injected.

Wrong Administration Technique Error

Case Report 050135. A child presented in the emergency department as a result of his mother administering an acetaminophen suppository with the foil wrapper still in place. No permanent harm to the patient was reported.

Discussion. This report shows that no situation is too far-fetched. Health care professionals need to be reminded that even the most unlikely mistakes can happen, whether in the home or in their organization. Patients and practitioners alike should constantly be reminded of the basics of proper medication administration and use (for example, removing a foil wrapper before inserting a suppository).

Deteriorated Drug Error

Case Report 050123. A vial of a clindamycin phosphate product was labeled by the manufacturer as "pharmacy bulk package, not for direct infusion." The labeling may have implied that this was a multidose vial, although it did not specify either single dose or multidose. In fine print on the back of the label, it read, "discard four hours after initial entry." The product was found stored in the refrigerator, dated when it was opened, and being used as a multidose vial beyond the four-hour period.

Discussion. A "pharmacy bulk package" is intended for use in a pharmacy admixture program. The closure is designed to be penetrated only once after reconstitution with a suitable sterile transfer device or dispensing set. It may not contain a substance to prevent the growth of microorganisms.[7] A high-volume, single-dose vial or a pharmacy bulk package should never be used as a multidose vial because it could result in drug deterioration.

Errors: Products, Processes, and People

The cases in the preceding section illustrate errors classified by specific causes (wrong dose, omission, and so forth), but classification can also be more generalized. As identified through the USP MER Program, errors fitting into three broad categories—products, processes, and people—warrant particular mention because of the frequency of occurrence or the severity of outcome. This section provides case reports highlighting some of these errors.

Product Errors

Those in human factors research would suggest that, when creating product names or designing products and labels, a type of failure mode analysis should be used. Such analysis presumes that, where humans are involved, it is not a matter of *if* an error will occur but *when*. Since the earliest days of the USP MER Program, the drug product or drug administration device has been an obvious cause of or contributor to reported errors. Attributes such as the brand name, generic name, labeling, packaging, and design have been cited as error-prone aspects of the product when it is placed in the medication use system. Some would choose to blame individual health care practitioners for not reading a label carefully, learning to use a device properly, or pronouncing a drug name properly, or converting a trade name to a generic name (and vice versa) correctly. Although

this may be the case in some circumstances, other situations can clearly be prevented through a small change to the product itself or its application in medication use.

Case Report 042212. Nursing staff on a long-term care/palliative care unit ordered Roxanol™ (morphine sulfate immediate release) concentrated oral solution (30-mL bottle) from the pharmacy. A 30-mL bottle of Roxicodone™ Intensol™ (oxycodone hydrochloride) was sent instead. The patient was administered seven doses of 60 mg of Roxicodone™ (instead of 60 mg of Roxanol™) over 2 days. The doses were administered by four different members of the nursing staff. Because 30 mg of oral oxycodone is roughly equivalent to 60 mg of oral morphine, the patient received the equivalent of twice the intended morphine dose on each occasion. The patient did not experience any adverse outcome. The error was discovered by a nurse who had made the same mistake (administering Roxicodone™ Intensol™ instead of Roxanol™) several weeks earlier.

Discussion. These errors may have occurred because the products have similar names (Roxanol™ versus Roxicodone™); are both packaged in 30-mL bottles; come in the same concentration (20 mg/mL); have the same color label with the same or similar font size and type; and are both clear, colorless solutions. Staff need to be reeducated about the products. The organization is trying to identify another source that uses different packaging and labeling for either of the products.

Issues such as these are one of the primary focuses of the USP and the Institute for Safe Medication Practices. Similarly labeled products are more likely to be confused for one another when their doses, names, and therapeutic uses are similar. Through the combined use of font size and type, layout, and color, a manufacturer can design more distinctive labels for its products, particularly if the company's overall packaging is identical among its products. Confusion is also compounded when a product is new to a practitioner or the marketplace, because practitioners experience confirmation bias—they see what they know. Storing such products in bins or on shelves remote from each other is helpful. Creating a "new products" shelf to aid practitioners in becoming accustomed to the products is standard practice in many facilities. It is also suggested that the manufacturers involved consider a name change.

Case Report 050131. A patient's husband took two prescriptions to the pharmacy. One was for Lasix® (furosemide, a diuretic) 40 mg. The pharmacist mistakenly dispensed Lanoxin® (digoxin, a cardiotonic) 0.25 mg instead. The patient intentionally compared the Lasix® tablets from her previous prescription with the tablets in the misfilled prescription. She did not discover the error because Lasix® 40 mg tablets and Lanoxin® 0.25 mg tablets are very similar in shape, color, and size. The patient took three tablets a day from the misfilled prescription. At the same time, she was also taking a regular maintenance dose of Lanoxin® 0.125 mg, and was therefore receiving 0.875 mg of Lanoxin® daily. Several weeks later, the patient was feeling ill, and her husband noticed that she had not been diuresing fluids as she should have been with the Lasix®. After examining the tablets with a magnifying glass, he determined that they were not Lasix®. The patient was taken to the emergency room for treatment.

Discussion. This particular type of product mix-up has been involved in several incidents reported to the USP MER Program. Often, the unclear handwriting of the prescriber is at fault (computerized order entry helps with this). For errors that slip through the usual safeguards, the patient or caregiver can provide a last check to validate a medication and detect an error. If the tablets or capsules are so similar that a patient needs a magnifying glass to distinguish between them, detecting an error may be unlikely. Although it would be unreasonable to expect every product from every manufacturer to look dissimilar, special care should be taken in the storage and handling of drugs used in a single patient population. In this case, the cardiotonic and diuretic are a common pair in drug therapy. Several mix-ups also have been reported by elderly patients who are confused, have poor vision, or take multiple prescription medications. Outpatient pharmacies should take special precautions to counsel patients thoroughly and label such drug combinations clearly and in a font size large enough for the elderly to read.

Case Report 041950. Staff first read the prescription shown in Figure 3-2 (page 49) as Ultram® (tramadol, an analgesic) 50 mg. After consulting with the patient and contacting the physician, it was determined to be Voltaren® (diclofenac, an anti-inflammatory) 50 mg. There had been other instances of near misses with these two medications. The prescribing physician's handwriting had been consistently illegible and it had been particularly difficult to distinguish these two drug names.

Discussion. Many of the errors in the USP MER Program database characterized as "unauthorized drug" involve drugs with similar names which lead to the wrong product being administered. The USP has compiled a list of nearly 700 drug names, both brand and generic, that have been reported to cause confusion.[8] Names can be confused as one brand for another, a brand for a generic, or one generic for another. The drug name also may be confused when spoken, handwritten, or read. Contributing factors include

- the accent or dialect of the individual speaking, mispronunciation, sound distortion during telephone conversations, or illegible handwriting;

Confusing Drug Names

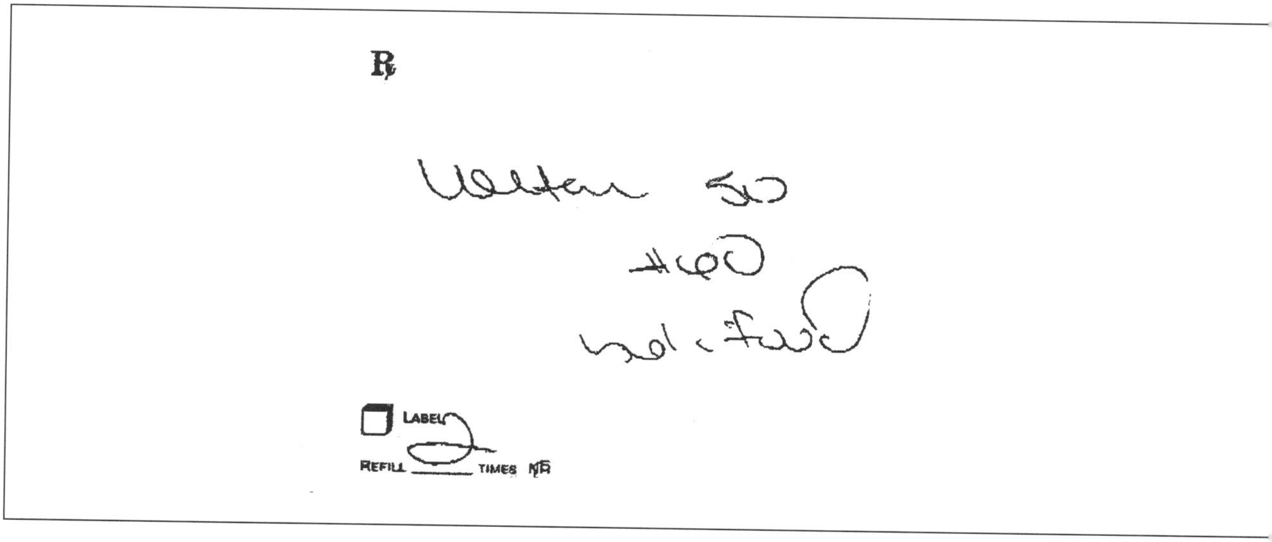

Figure 3-2. *This prescription, written for the anti-inflammatory Voltaren®, was misread as the analgesic Ultram®.*
Source: USP Medication Errors Reporting Program, Rockville, MD. Case 041950. Used with permission.

- similarly named drugs available in the same strength;

- similarly named drugs with the same indication for use;

- misleading similar packaging or labeling that encourages the misreading of the drug name;

- knowledge deficits; and

- confirmation bias (identifying a drug name as one with which the practitioner is familiar).

To avoid drug name errors, verbal orders should be avoided (or prohibited). Where this is not possible, drug names should be repeated and spelled aloud for all verbal orders. The drug name should be clearly printed or typed on the medication order; all illegible orders should be checked with the prescriber, and computerized order entry should be used whenever possible. Products with similar names should be kept apart in stock rooms. Drug orders should be as complete as possible and include the strength, indication for use, and dosing.

Case Report 041000. An outpatient chemotherapy prescription was written by a physician as "6 mercaptopurine 50 mg QD [every day]." The pharmacy technician interpreted the order as "take 6 mercaptopurine tablets daily" rather than "take one 6-mercaptopurine tablet daily." The pharmacist discovered the error when verifying the information on the prescription.

Discussion. Suffixes and prefixes can be misinterpreted, misunderstood, or simply omitted on an order. Furthermore, definitions of suffixes are not standardized. It has been suggested that drug suffixes be eliminated from drug names.

Chemical names (for example, 5-fluorouracil, 6-mercaptopurine) should never be used in place of generic names.

Case Report 41976. An elderly patient on glipizide (for diabetes) purchased Anacin® (contains aspirin) instead of Anacin-3® (contains acetaminophen in place of aspirin). The similarity of the names reportedly caused the confusion. She took one tablet three times a day for knee pain for several weeks. When the patient complained of dizzy spells to the pharmacist, she was advised to discontinue the Anacin® because "aspirin displaces glipizide from protein binding, thereby increasing the blood concentration of glipizide."

Discussion. Added care should be taken in using over-the-counter medications and in recommending them to patients. Mix-ups have been reported in health care facilities as well as in the home.[8] Labels must be read carefully, and staff and patients educated regarding product differences.

Case Report 041288. Twelve ready-to-use, premixed bags of a neuromuscular blocking agent were brought to a hospital pharmacy by the anesthesia technician responsible for monitoring pharmacy supplies in the surgery area. The bags had been lying on a table in the anesthesia break room of the main surgical area for some time, and none of the staff knew what to do with them. The technician later recovered 24 more bags of the same product from the anesthesia area of the ambulatory surgery center. On investigation, it was determined that a sales representative apparently asked one of the anesthesiologists to sign a receipt for 24 units of the drug. Because a total of 36 units were recovered, the technician realized that far more of this product had been left at the hospital than was indicated on the receipt signed by the physician. There was no way to confirm whether any bags were used on patients or whether additional bags had been left somewhere in the surgery storage areas.

Discussion. The entry of drugs into any facility should be strictly controlled by a process administered in the pharmacy. Strict controls provide accountability for units used; recovery of units in the event of a recall; and proper training for use of new dosage forms, strengths, delivery systems, and so on.

Case Report 042031. An order was written for cyclosporine oral solution 30 mg to be administered to a pediatric patient. However, a nurse, believing that the syringe was calibrated in mg and not mL, administered several doses of 300 mg. The oral solution is available as 100 mg/mL. As the pharmacist reviewed the error, he noted that the syringes (see Figure 3-3, page 51) accompanying the medication were never designed with pediatrics in mind. It is not possible to administer any dose less than 0.5 mL or 50 mg. He thought it was understandable that the nurse assumed that the "3" mark was for 30 mg—it is positioned between "2,5" and "3,5" (which are European expressions for the decimals 2.5 and 3.5). To harmonize products in the global market, the manufacturer chose to follow the European Convention for expressing numbers which uses commas and decimals in the reverse manner as in the U.S. (for example 1,000 mL in U.S. is 1.000 mL in Europe).

Discussion. This error is unusual in that it involves global trade issues. Manufacturers would prefer to harmonize products used here with those available in other markets. If dose preparation is centralized in the pharmacy, this kind of error might be avoided.

Other medication errors involving medication dispensing devices reported to USP have included the interchange of devices supplied with specific products. Each device packaged with a medication is calibrated for that medication based on the viscosity and concentration of the specific liquid

Packaged Measuring Device

Figure 3-3. *The markings on this syringe, packaged with cyclosporine, led a nurse to believe that "3" meant 30 mg because of its placement between 2,5 and 3,5, which is a European method for expressing decimal placement.*

Source: USP Medication Errors Reporting Program, Rockville, MD. Case 042031. Used with permission.

it delivers. Often, the devices are not calibrated in any standardized way. Some measure in milligrams (mg), others in milliliters (mL), and others in cubic centimeters (cc). Still others have calibrations for the strength per drop or per teaspoonful. Policies should be in place so that the dispensing or use of droppers or calibrated cups provided with specific medications are restricted to those medications.

Process Errors
Each medication use process is a complex set of interrelated and interdependent tasks that may or may not be executed with accompanying

safeguards. The anatomy of an error that reaches the patient often reveals that more than a single mistake by a lone individual occurred in the systematic network of processes. It is likely that the error was the culmination of a series of errors in judgment, performance deficits, and knowledge deficits, each coupled with a weak or nonexistent safety mechanism. Examples of such mechanisms include checking for drug interactions, allergies, and contraindications; verifying drug name, strength, and dose; and using computerized patient information and order-entry systems.

Case Report 041021. A physician wrote an order for hydralazine (an antihypertensive) instead of hydroxyzine to control a patient's itching. The error was caught prior to administration to the patient. To help avoid future mix-ups, the organization now stocks hydroxyzine only in capsule form; hydralazine comes only in tablets.

Discussion. Prescription writing errors may be made by any health care professional with prescriptive authority. Computerized drug and patient information systems can help to deter such errors and should be implemented wherever possible. The system should include checks for dosage ranges, gender, age, drug and food interactions, and contraindications. Patient counseling also is an excellent safety net. In a study by the Indian Health Service, 83% of errors were discovered at the patient counseling phase of dispensing the medication.[9]

Case Report 41072. A physician ordered cisplatin as *100* mg/m^2 *over* 4 days per a protocol published in a cancer chemotherapy handbook. The protocol should have read *25* mg/m^2 daily *for* 4 days. The publisher had announced the error in an earlier memo, enclosing a label showing the correct dosage to be pasted over the incorrect statement. Unfortunately, the correction label had not been pasted in the book the physician used. The patient developed ototoxicity and eventually renal failure, and died.

Discussion. The tragedy of inaccuracies in published protocols, reference books, and electronic references is that the health care practitioner recognizes his or her own knowledge deficit, uses these resources to ascertain information, and then is misled. Such latent errors[10] are accidents waiting to happen and set up the individual to err. References should be chosen for reliability and currency. Incorrect references need to be removed from circulation as quickly as possible. All published protocols should be verified. A practitioner who has no knowledge of a product and its use should check two references (and discuss use with a colleague). Critical drugs, especially those for chemotherapy, should only be handled by individuals who are certified or generally knowledgeable about the products and therapies.

Case Report 050096. A patient received 70 units of Humulin ® 70/30, instead of 50 units. The patient became hypoglycemic but recovered following administration of orange juice, dextrose 50%, and D$_5$W (dextrose 5% in water). Blood glucose monitoring was increased. The error was due to the incorrect transcription of the order onto the computerized medication administration record. The system (an internal process) allowed order entry by the unit clerk without requiring double-checking by a registered nurse. The order was for "Insulin 70/30 Human 50 units q AM, 30 units q PM." The clerk entered the dosage as "70 units in AM and 30 units in PM." He or she might have looked at the first time of day specified on the order and assumed that 70/30 meant the patient's daily insulin dosages.

Discussion. Computerization may generally be viewed as an opportunity to routinize tasks such as order transcription so professional staff can concentrate their efforts elsewhere. A facility may be more likely to use support staff to perform these tasks. However, order-entry processes should not be overly simplified and should be carried out by appropriately trained staff with health care professionals conducting the process checks. Software programs should incorporate forcing functions such as double entry of the key elements of a medication order or confirming the order with a prompt ("Are you sure?"). Staff members need to train themselves to remain sensitized to such programming and to use it as a final chance to confirm key data elements such as dose. Computer programmers should restrict the use of such force functions to the most important data elements.

Case Report 042186. An order faxed to a pharmacy for VP16 (VePesid ®; etoposide, an antineoplastic) 150 mg was interpreted incorrectly and filled with VP16 180 mg. The physician had used a roller-ball pen when writing the order, which made 150 look like 180 (see Figure 3-4, page 54). When a copy of the order arrived at the pharmacy, it showed the correct dose. The patient received three doses, but no adverse outcome was reported.

Discussion. The causes of transcription errors can be elusive. Use of abbreviations coupled with poor penmanship can set the stage for errors. A lack of drug knowledge on the part of the transcriber can cause him or her to misread a drug name due to confirmation bias. Many errors at this stage can be avoided by using preprinted order sheets, printing instead of handwriting orders, staff members checking each other's work, and computerizing order entry. Misinterpretations due to the poor readability (or deceptive clarity) of faxed prescriptions and misinterpretations caused by the use of felt-tip or roller-ball pens have been reported in enough cases to suggest reevaluation of their use in the prescribing process.

Human Errors

Human factors engineers and cognitive behavior specialists have long sought to identify the reasons for human error. Part of the answer may be that humans develop skills that enable them to perform by rote. The comfort level with this "autopilot" stage of activity reflects learned patterns of performance that require little thought. In this mode, any diversion of attention may result in unintended actions. On the other hand, variations in task complexities often require that rules be developed and applied in changing situations, or that expertise be learned and applied to unfamiliar situations in the most complex of tasks.[11] The formal training of health care professionals is focused on

developing rule- and knowledge-based behaviors. Experienced individuals evolve to be able to operate in skill-based performance modes by developing patterns of operation in their work. Because individuals are operating within a system, certain performance-shaping factors, such as a heavy workload, inadequate workspace, or poor lighting, can influence human performance.[11]

As illustrated by the case reports throughout this chapter, errors are not confined to new employees, recent graduates, float staff, and support staff. Seasoned individuals performing tasks within the medication use system can be just as prone to error. Patients and nonmedical caregivers also play an important role as the final safety checks in the drug therapy chain, especially when they are asked to take on added responsibilities for complex therapies provided in the home. Building their skill sets and imparting rules and knowledge to them is an important part of safe and proper medication use.

The cases that follow have no subsequent discussion. Efforts at ongoing and consistent communication and education are usually the most effective means to reducing human error.

Case Report 050100. A child with a diagnosis of leukemia was initially discharged with a nasogastric tube for intermittent enteral supplemental feedings. The child was readmitted for routine chemotherapy and developed an infection. A peripherally inserted central catheter (PICC) line was placed for administration of IV antibiotics at home. When the PICC line clotted, the mother, having been taught to unclog the child's nasogastric tube with ginger ale, assumed that this method could probably be used for all tubes. Fortunately, the home care nurse arrived just as the mother had drawn up the ginger ale into the syringe. Obviously, an IV injection of ginger ale could have been fatal.

Transcription Error

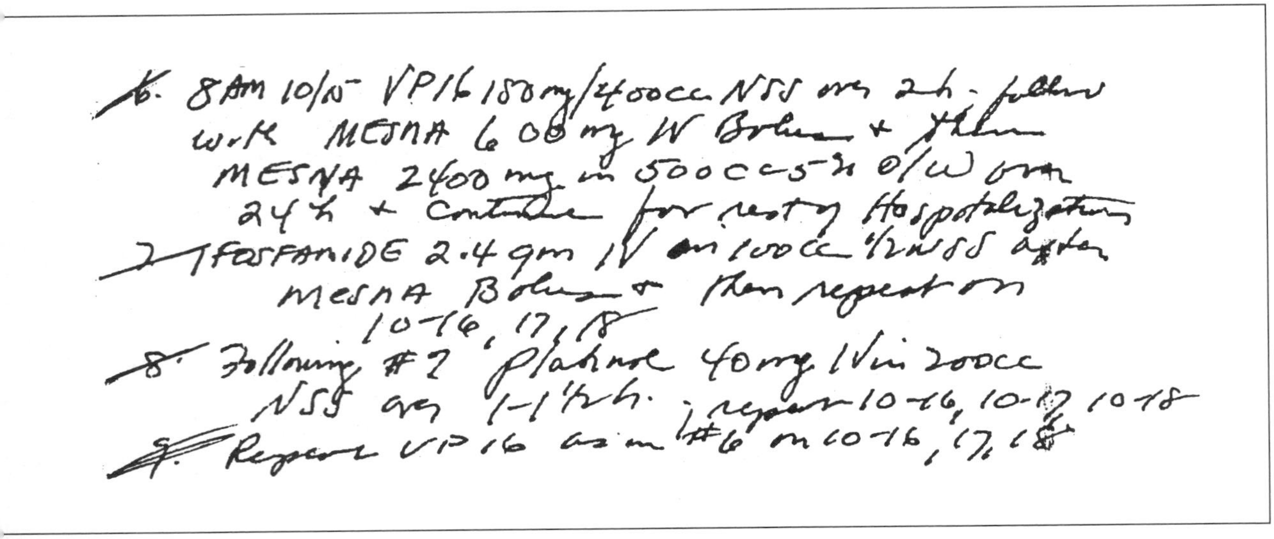

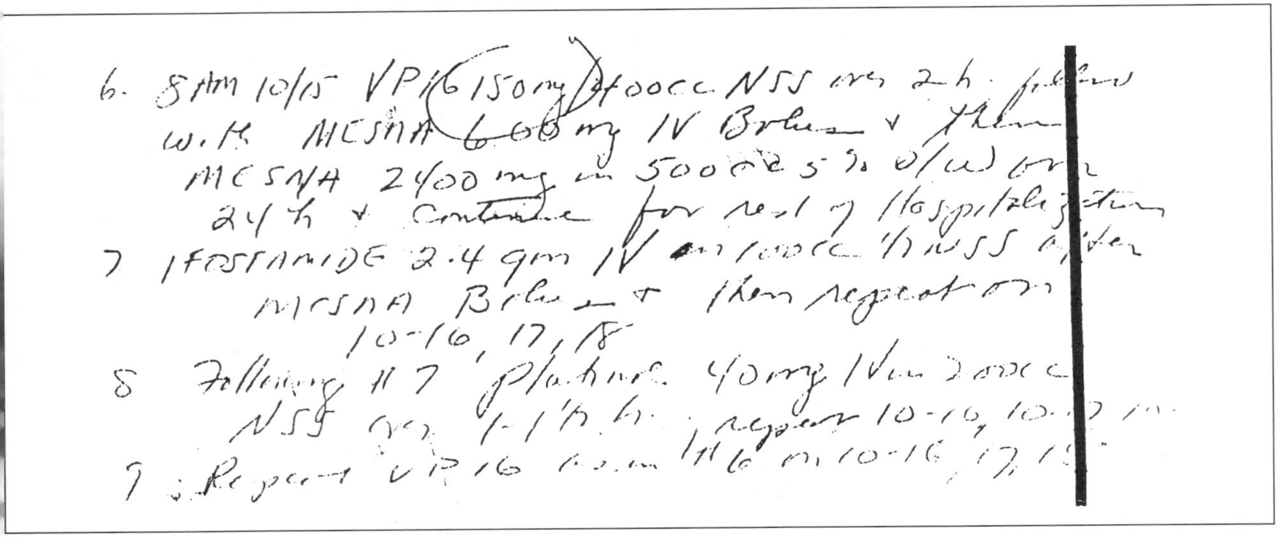

Figure 3-4. *This order was written with a roller-ball pen and faxed to the pharmacy (top of the page). The strength of VP16 (etoposide) was misread as 180 mg. A copy of the original order (directly above) was sent to the pharmacy later. The dose on this copy is clearly 150 mg.*

Source: USP Medication Errors Reporting Program, Rockville, MD. Case 042186. Used with permission.

Case Report 041816. An infectious disease physician wrote an order for three medications to be given TIW. He reasoned that if *TID* means three times a day, *TIW* must mean three times a week. The order was sent with the patient from the physician's office to the hospital. The nurse at the hospital was unfamiliar with TIW and presumed it meant TID (three times daily). Uncomfortable with this dose, she checked with the physician and identified the error. The pharmacy has now developed a list of approved abbreviations to avoid similar errors.

Case Report 050001. A hospital pharmacy had dispensed a box of ten 5-mL vials of 5 mg/mL concentration of Versed ® instead of the usual 1 mg/mL concentration. The concentrations are distinguished by the use of color on the vials, but the manufacturer's cartons for both strengths have the same blue-and-white color scheme. The nurse in the endoscopy suite would routinely withdraw 5 mL of the 1 mg/mL concentration for the physician to administer to patients. The nurse usually on the unit was not available and the substitute nurse did not notice the distinctive green label on the vial. A patient received 25 mg instead of 5 mg of Versed ® (midazolam), but experienced no adverse effects.

Automation: Pros and Cons

Computerized order-entry systems have been cited several times in this chapter as possible solutions for certain types of medication errors, such as illegible orders. Automation of all kinds can incorporate controls to check patient information such as gender, age, allergies, concurrent drug therapy, dosing calculations, drug interactions, and contraindications.

However, all automated systems also possess some degree of fallibility. In fact, automation often lulls individuals into a false sense of security with regard to consistency, accuracy, and dependability. Even with the most sophisticated machine, the element of operator error is a contributing factor. For example, in one case (042257) reported to the USP MER Program, a normally pleasant patient became agitated, confused, and aphasic when a 5-mg tablet of methylphenidate (a stimulant) was erroneously administered in place of a 5-mg tablet of metolazone (a diuretic). A registered nurse entered the name of the wrong medication into the automated medication dispensing system. Luckily, only one dose was given before the error was discovered.

In another case (041788), a pharmacy technician filled a Pyxis machine drawer in the surgical intensive care unit with vials of gentamicin instead of vials of potassium chloride concentrate for injection. The pharmacist did not double-check the machine after it had been restocked. Four different nurses gave the gentamicin to four different patients (presuming it was potassium chloride).

Automated equipment and devices, including computers, cannot be used in an autopilot mode. The individuals who operate these systems need to be trained properly and schooled sufficiently to be able to detect latent errors. The American Society of Health-System Pharmacists is developing guidelines for the use of automated dispensing equipment which should be useful in the development of organizationwide policies. Care should be taken to select reliable vendors of pharmacy dispensing systems software. Programming designed within the facility should include a review by a health care professional to check functionality such as dosing calculations, contraindications and allergy alerts, and links to appropriate patient information.

Reducing Medication Errors

A facility's medication error reporting system should define "medication error" in its broadest sense. This includes identifying potential errors and determining the frequency of occurrence, severity of potential consequences, and the cost to modify the medication use system.

Identifying the causes of medication errors is not always as easy as it may seem. The medication use system is a set of complex, interdependent processes performed by students and licensed health care professionals, support staff, and patients and their caregivers. The causes of errors are innumerable and the solutions require multidisciplinary cooperation. The most obvious cause of error (including the individual who erred) is never the root cause; each occurrence needs to be analyzed thoroughly. Small changes to any one process can effect signif-

icant incremental improvements in the system. However, adjustments can also create new opportunities for error. Change should be implemented cautiously. This emphasizes the importance of studying any changes to the system and making adjustments where necessary.

Various strategies may be employed to prevent and reduce the frequency of errors. For example, demands on participants in the medication use system should be compatible with their capabilities, limitations, experience, and expectations.[11] Staff should be made aware of types and causes of medication errors to enable them to better anticipate error. Chapter 4 provides an in-depth discussion of prevention strategies.

References

1. ASHP Report: Guidelines on preventing medication errors in hospitals. *ASHP* 50:305–314, Feb 1993.

2. Barker KN, Kimbrough WW, Heller WM: *A Study of Medication Errors in a Hospital.* Fayetteville: University of Arkansas, 1966.

3. Allan EL, Barker KN: Fundamentals of medication error research. *Am J Hosp Pharm* 47:555–571, 1990.

4. U.S. Pharmacopeia: National council focuses on coordinating medication error reduction efforts. *USP Quality Review,* Jan 1997, p 57.

5. Edgar TA, Lee DS, Cousins DD: Experience with a national medication error reporting program. *Am J Hosp Pharm* 51:1335–1338, 1994.

6. Leape LL: Error in medicine. *JAMA* 272:1851–1857, 1994.

7. U.S. Pharmacopeia: *USP XXIII-NF XVIII.* Rockville, MD: U.S. Pharmacopeial Convention, 1995.

8. U.S. Pharmacopeia: OTC names: An invitation to err? *USP Quality Review,* May 1996, p 56.

9. Kuyper AR: Patient counseling detects prescription errors. *Hosp Pharm* 28:12, 1993.

10. Reason J: *Human Error.* Cambridge, MA: Cambridge University Press, 1992.

Chapter 4:

PREVENTING MEDICATION ERRORS

David W Bates, MD, MSc
Assistant Professor of Medicine, Harvard Medical School
Medical Director, Brigham and Woman's Physician Hospital Organization
Boston, Massachusetts

In previous chapters, we have seen that errors can occur at any stage of the medication use system, whether it is prescribing and selection, preparing and dispensing, administering, or monitoring. To prevent medication errors, it is necessary to know what errors are occurring where and how the system *should* operate. This chapter discusses the key strategies for preventing medication errors. To evaluate the effectiveness of prevention strategies, the error rate must be measured. Previous chapters have focused on measuring and monitoring processes within the medication use system and defining the errors that can occur. This chapter begins with a brief discussion of measurement studies as they relate to the theory of error prevention. The bulk of the discussion, however, deals with general and specific prevention strategies that can be used in various health care settings.

Measurement and Prevention Studies

Medication errors are common, although their frequency as measured in studies depends heavily upon the definition used, the clinical setting, and the methods used to look for them.[1] For example, Allan and Barker[2] defined medication error as "a deviation from the physician's medication order as written in the chart," which excludes errors at the ordering stage. Barker has performed a series of observation-based studies in which a trained observer watches a health care professional, notes what he or she does when administering drugs, and watches the patient receive the medication.[2] This approach identifies about one medication error per patient per day, and is reliable; it represents an effective mechanism for identifying administration errors.[3]

Other researchers have evaluated ordering errors intercepted by pharmacists.[4,5] In one study, Folli found 4.7 errors per 1,000 orders at two children's hospitals.[5] In another, Lesar found 3.1 errors per 1,000 orders at a teaching hospital.[4] Of these, 58% were judged to have the potential for adverse consequences. Such an approach is a valuable source of "near misses." It can detect areas in which prevention mechanisms can be implemented before patient harm occurs, and is relatively easy to maintain. Its shortcomings are that administration and dispensing errors cannot be assessed, and it does not allow estimation of adverse drug event (ADE) rates or of the number of errors affecting patients.

The Relationship Between Medication Errors, Adverse Drug Events, and Potential Adverse Drug Events

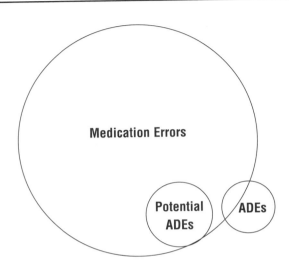

Figure 4-1. *Only a small proportion of medication errors represent an adverse drug event (ADE) or a potential ADE. Although all potential ADEs are medication errors, only a small number of ADEs are associated with medication errors.*

Source: Bates DW, et al: Relationship Between Medication Errors and Adverse Drug Events. *J Gen Intern Med* 10(4):201. Used with permission.

Yet another approach is to evaluate not only intercepted ordering errors, but those resulting in harm. One study which did this identified errors through a review of all orders by a trained individual and self-reporting by pharmacy staff; ADEs were identified primarily by chart review.[6] The study took place on three medical units in a tertiary care hospital. Among 10,070 medication orders, there were 530 medication errors, 25 ADEs (of which 5 were preventable), and 35 potential ADEs. Thus, about 1 in 100 medication errors resulted in a preventable ADE, and there were 7 times as many potential ADEs (Figure 4-1, above). Among the errors attributed not to missing doses, 82% were estimated to be potentially preventable using physician order entry. Although this approach provided valuable information about how many medication errors result in ADEs, routine chart review is too expensive to do on a routine basis.

From these examples and as emphasized in Chapter 3, it should be clear that comparisons between medication error rates are only meaningful if the definitions of error are similar and the error identification approaches are described. Indeed, van Leeuwen[7] evaluated the reporting rates of medication errors by pharmacies in a national health system and found tremendous variation; these data argue convincingly that measures cannot be used to make interorganization comparisons unless the same measures and data collection methods are used. This may be accomplished by participating in an external measurement system with defined measures. Even without such participation, measuring medication error rates should be useful within organizations, and measurement of rates is vital for demonstrating the effectiveness of prevention strategies.

Patient injuries due to drugs are common in acute care, ambulatory care, and long term care settings. Historically, most studies have used the adverse drug reaction (ADR) as the outcome, and many have evaluated the frequency of ADRs in hospitalized patients.[8–18] However, the true incidence of drug injuries is controversial and varies widely (1.5% to 35%) depending upon the strategy used to identify them.[19] Because an ADR as defined by the World Health Organization excludes injuries due to errors, the term "adverse drug event" has advantages for organizations trying to reduce error rates, because it includes both preventable and nonpreventable adverse drug events.

In the ADE Prevention Study, in medical and surgical patients in two tertiary care hospitals in the United States, the overall ADE rate was 6.5 per 100 admissions.[20] Of these ADEs, 28% were judged preventable and were thus associated with a medication error. Moreover, many of these ADEs appeared preventable by changing the systems involved.[21] Fewer data are available about ADEs in the ambulatory care and long term care settings, but studies are ongoing. It is clear that drug injuries have important economic consequences. Johnson and Bootman have estimated the annual cost of drug-related morbidity and mortality in the United States at $77 billion, with $47 billion related to hospital admissions due to drug therapy or the absence of appropriate drug therapy.[22]

Theory of Error in Relation to Medication Errors

Outside health care, experts have found that the most common cause of defects is the production process itself, not the individuals within it.[23,24] Berwick,[25] Laffel and Blumenthal,[26] and Leape[27] have taken the position that this idea applies in health care as well. According to the philosophy of total quality management, the true cause of an accident is not viewed simply as a "human error,"

but as the result of a system that allowed an operator error to result in an accident.

Leape has recently written about error in medicine, and has made the point that errors are an everyday occurrence, and that everyone makes many daily.[27] Fortunately, most errors have few irrevocable consequences, but errors in medication use can be harmful. Though traditional medical systems have focused on finding bad practitioners, or "bad apples," particularly when medications are involved, most errors are made by competent practitioners. In evaluating 264 serious medication errors (those which either injured or had the potential to injure a patient), Leape, et al identified no instances in which there was a pattern of repeated error by an individual.[21] These data suggest that effective prevention strategies should focus primarily on the systems for giving drugs, and only secondarily on the individuals involved in the process.

General Recommendations for Preventing Medication Errors

Any approach for preventing medication errors should use a systems perspective, and consider the entire process of giving medications.[21] Approaches that focus attention on the individuals who commit errors are likely to be counterproductive, encouraging employees to hide mistakes and sabotaging data collection efforts for performance improvement. Nonetheless, it is necessary to have ways to identify the rare individuals who exhibit a pattern of repeated errors, and the reasons for poor performance of such individuals should be investigated.

Systems should be designed both to make errors less likely and to intercept those that do occur. Some key prevention strategies that emerged from systems analysis of medication errors are to

- minimize reliance on memory;

- improve access to reliable drug information;

- introduce "error-proofing" or development of systems that eliminate the possibility of error, when possible;

- pursue standardization within organizations; and

- provide training in the systems involved.[21]

One example of error-proofing comes from anesthesia; at one point, there were a number of reports of anoxic brain injury because a gas other than oxygen had been fixed to the oxygen nozzle during surgery. The error-proofing approach was to change the oxygen yoke, so that no other gas could be given through it. Training, retraining for new technology or processes, and continuing education are essential, but are sometimes left behind; although they are not discussed as specific educational strategies, they are important for preventing medication errors, particularly for the introduction of new technologies, such as intravenous pumps or medications.

The National Coordinating Council for Medication Error Reporting and Prevention (MERP) has made a number of general recommendations about preventing errors in prescription writing:[28]

- *All prescription documents must be legible.* Prescribers should move to a direct, computerized order-entry system.

- *Prescribers should avoid the use of abbreviations, including those for drug names (for example, MOM, HCTZ) and Latin directions for use.* The abbreviations in Table 4-1 (page 61) have been found to be particularly dangerous because they have been consistently misunderstood. The Council reviewed the uses for many abbreviations and determined that any attempt at standardization would not adequately address the problems of illegibility and misuse.

- *Prescription orders should include a brief notation of purpose (for example, for cough), unless considered inappropriate by the prescriber.* Notation of purpose can help further ensure that the proper medication is dispensed and creates an extra safety check in the process. The Council does recognize, however, that certain medications and disease states may warrant maintaining confidentiality.

- *All prescription orders should be written in the metric system except for therapies such as insulin, vitamins, and so on that use standard units. The word "units" should be spelled out rather than written as "U."* The change to the use of the metric system from the archaic apothecary and avoirdupois systems will help avoid misinterpretations of these abbreviations and symbols, as well as miscalculations when converting to metric, which is used in product labeling and package inserts.

- *Prescribers should include the age and, when appropriate, weight of the patient on the prescription or medication order.* The most common errors in dosage occur in pediatric and geriatric populations in which low body weight is common. The age (and weight) of a patient can help dispensing health care professionals in their double-check of the appropriate drug and dose.

- *Prescribers should not use vague instructions such as "Take as directed" or "Take/Use as needed" as the sole direction for use.* Specific directions to the patient are useful to help reinforce proper medication use, particularly if therapy is to be interrupted for a time. Clear directions are a necessity for the dispenser to

  - check the proper dose for the patient and

  - enable effective patient counseling.

- *The medication order should include drug name, exact metric weight or concentration, and dosage form.* Strength should be expressed in metric amounts and concentration should be specified. Each

Table 4-1. Dangerous Abbreviations Involved in Medication Errors

Abbreviation	Intended Meaning	Common Error
U	Units	Mistaken as a zero or a four (4) resulting in overdose. Also mistaken for "cc" (cubic centimeters) when poorly written
µg	Micrograms	Mistaken for "mg" (milligrams) resulting in overdose
QD	Latin abbreviation for every day	The period after the "Q" has sometimes been mistaken for an "I", and the drug has been given "QID" (four times daily) rather than daily
QOD	Latin abbreviation for every other day	Misinterpreted as "QD" (daily) or "QID" (four times daily). If the "O" is poorly written, it looks like a period or "I"
SC or SQ	Subcutaneous	Mistaken as "SL" (sublingual) when poorly written
TIW	Three times a week	Misinterpreted as "three times a day" or "twice a week"
D/C	Discharge; also discontinue	Patient's medications have been prematurely discontinued when D/C, (intended to mean "discharge") was misinterpreted as "discontinue," because it was followed by a list of drugs
HS	Half strength	Misinterpreted as the Latin abbreviation "HS" (hour of sleep)
cc	Cubic centimeters	Mistaken as "U" (units) when poorly written
AU, AS, AD	Latin abbreviation for both ears; left ear; right ear	Misinterpreted as the Latin abbreviation "OU" (both eyes); "OS" (left eye); "OD" (right eye)

Source: National Coordinating Council for Medication Error Reporting and Prevention, Rockville, MD.

order for a medication should be complete. The pharmacist should check with the prescriber if any information is missing or questionable.

- *A leading zero should always precede a decimal expression of less than one.* A terminal or trailing zero should never be used after a decimal. Tenfold errors in drug strength and dosage have occurred with decimals due to the use of a trailing zero or the absence of a leading zero.

Medication errors are common, although only about one in a hundred results in an injury. Of adverse drug events in hospitals, about 30% are associated with a medication error and are pre-

ventable.[20] Depending upon the resources available to the organization, a variety of measures may improve safety. For organizations with little computerization, changing the roles of pharmacists and implementing computerized order checking in the pharmacy are likely to be effective. In the longer term, organizations will want to move to computerized ordering systems, in which providers write orders online so that decision support can be provided.

Specific Prevention Strategies

Specific error prevention strategies aimed at systems improvement can be extremely productive.

So can efforts to enhance education and training, teamwork, self-assessment, and information management. Proactive efforts in each of these areas can reduce and prevent medication errors. Systems improvement can be obtained by targeting any of the processes in the following section.

Unit-Dose Dispensing

Unit dosing has been highly effective at reducing the frequency of medication errors, as was initially demonstrated in the 1970s.[29,30] In unit-dose dispensing, doses are individually packaged and sent to the point of use for specific patients, rather than relying on floor stock. In one study, unit-dose dispensing reduced the frequency of medication errors by a remarkable 82%,[30] including reducing wrong dose errors (which accounted for 73% of errors in the control phase), extra dose errors, and unordered drug errors. Some of the reasons unit dosing works so well are as follows:

- Designed into the process is interdependency among the prescriber, pharmacist and nurse. No one of these professionals can execute the process from beginning to end without checks by others.

- All medication orders are reviewed for appropriateness and completeness by a pharmacist before the first dose is prescribed.

- Medications are provided in the exact dose needed and in a fully labeled package that retains its labeling to the point of use.

- Each dose of medication is packaged ready to administer; no further mixing or manipulation is required.

- Doses are prepared and provided to those administering doses so that the currency of the medication and dose is reliable. Thus, it is not a medication or dose that was right three days ago, but is correct at the time it is administered to the patient.

Unit dosing remains an effective strategy for medication error prevention.[1]

Targeted Provider Education

A variety of methods have been used to attempt to change physicians' medication-related decision-making behavior, including dissemination of printed information, group lectures, drug-utilization audits, one-on-one educational efforts by clinical pharmacists, and required consultation or justification prior to use.[31] Education about new drugs, dosage forms, and delivery devices is important, although much of this learning still occurs "on the job" from other physicians or from detailers from pharmaceutical companies. While educational strategies are generally effective in the short term, they have had little long-term effect, primarily because continuing reinforcement is required. Although mandatory consultations are effective, they are costly and intrusive, and their effects continue only as long as they are maintained. Clinical pharmacy consultative services reduce error rates,[32] but are labor-intensive, and most have focused primarily on a few drugs with narrow toxic-therapeutic levels.

Nonetheless, education is essential for changing beliefs about prescribing behavior. Clinicians are often unwilling to make drug changes based on computerized information alone in situations in which they have strongly held beliefs, although they readily accept suggestions about dose and frequency changes.[33] Thus, clinical counter detailing—one-on-one encounters primarily between clinical pharmacists and practitioners to convince practitioners about the merits of specific controversial changes such as once-daily aminoglycoside dosing—will likely be important. However, more minor changes and long-term maintenance will likely occur through computerized systems, which are less expensive.

Role Changes for Pharmacists

For many years, physicians have made most decisions about drug therapy for patients with relatively little input from pharmacists, who have a great deal to contribute. When based in the central pharmacy, however, pharmacists are in a reactive role and often have relatively little clinical information available to them. The concept of having pharmacists function as members of the patient care team is not new, but it has received relatively little study.[34-37] Nonetheless, it is very attractive, particularly in clinical settings with intensive drug therapy such as intensive care units and hematology-oncology units. The number of health care organizations which are providing clinical pharmacy services has risen.[38] In 1992, 67% of hospitals nationally reported that pharmacists were involved in managing ADRs, but in only 18% of hospitals did pharmacists participate regularly in medical rounds.[38] A number of studies suggest that pharmacists can intercept large numbers of medication errors.[4,5,34] For example, Folli et al found that pharmacists intercepted 479 errors among 111,022 orders[5] at two children's hospitals. As in many other studies, the most common type of error was incorrect dosage. More data about the impact of clinical pharmacy services on outcomes such as medication error rates, costs, and length of stay will help justify these services.

In the ambulatory care setting, pharmacists have increased the amount of patient counseling about medications. This could be even more effective if additional clinical data were available to them, which should be possible as integrated delivery systems develop better information systems. State pharmacy practice acts and federal regulations require "an offer to counsel," yet pharmacies are not doing enough of this, probably in part because there are few opportunities to do so. With increasing penetration of managed care, this could change.

In long term care, monthly pharmacist visits are mandated, and pharmacists play a key role in evaluating the medication regimens of the frail elderly. With time, it may be useful for them to become even more proactive in this role; currently, they question orders in the record but rarely call physicians directly, partly because it is difficult to contact them and also because physicians are often unreceptive when contacted.

Computerized Pharmacy Checking

The process of computerized pharmacy checking, in which orders are entered in the pharmacy and then checked for drug allergies, drug–drug interactions, appropriateness of dosing and frequency, and other problems, is widely used and relatively easy to implement compared to physician order entry (see page 64). Several commercially available products, such as FirstDatabank, Micromedex, and Medispan, provide these and a number of other checks, and such companies continuously update their data, which is a major task for an individual organization. In general, computers excel at inspection, while humans inevitably make many errors. Although few data are available about the effectiveness of this approach, computerized pharmacy checking should intercept many errors.

It does, however, have limitations. The pharmacist has to notify the physician if there is a problem. This can be difficult, because the pharmacist may not be able to rapidly identify the physician or the physician may not respond rapidly and may be irritated when notified. The pharmacist has to decide whether or not to call with relatively little patient-specific knowledge, and often under considerable production pressure in today's health care environment. Because of this pressure, pharmacists undoubtedly sometimes dispense a medication against their better judgment. Another vital issue is that the computerized error detection system not be set at too low a threshold; if it sends too many messages, especially messages that fail to result in change, the pharmacist may begin to ignore it as a coping mechanism. One recent study suggests that this may be occurring.[39] When prescriptions for two drugs with a life-threatening interaction were taken to 50 pharmacies, 16 pharmacies filled the orders without comment even though a computerized checking system was in place at 48 of the 50 pharmacies.

These problems notwithstanding, this approach is likely to be effective and is relatively easy to implement. It is feasible in the short run for outpatient pharmacies and for small health care organizations without sophisticated information systems.

Computerized Physician Order Entry

Although many U.S. health care organizations have in place computerized order entry by unit secretaries and nurses, less than 5% have implemented computerized physician order entry, in which clinicians write orders directly online for all orders.[40] Clerk order entry has serious disadvantages: transcription is required, with the associated opportunity for error, particularly because clerks may not be trained in drug names, doses, and administration routes, and, more importantly, the principal advantage of order entry—the ability to deliver messages to the orderer in real time—is lost. Physician order entry has been successful in a number of sites,[33,40] and has also decreased overall drug utilization in a randomized controlled trial.[41]

Physician order entry can decrease the frequency of medication errors in a number of ways.[33] Orders are legible, and input is structured, so that a drug name, dose, route, and frequency can be required for all orders. Because most orders are written using menus, error rates can be expected to fall because prescribers are choosing from a set

in which appropriate options are presented. Furthermore, orders can be subjected to a series of checks to look for drug allergies, drug–drug interactions, drug–laboratory problems, and drug dose problems, including daily, weekly or even life-time dose limits. Also, dosing guidelines for specific drugs such as aminoglycosides and heparin can be displayed, and the computer can calculate doses and recommend monitoring for these agents, which have been found to improve outcomes for some drugs such as heparin.[42] While several studies have documented the potential of computerized physician order entry for reducing the number of medication errors and drug injuries,[6,43] it is not yet clear how many such errors and injuries will be prevented, although studies to evaluate this are underway.

Standardization of Processes and Equipment

In industry, standardization of processes and equipment has been enormously effective in quality improvement. While few data are available from medicine, it is likely that similar benefits may be available. Examples of standardization which may reduce medication errors include limiting the number of different types of intravenous pumps, limiting the number of concentrations of medications such as dopamine, and standardizing the use of scales for drugs such as potassium, magnesium, and insulin. Drug formularies are an example of standardization, and use of only a few agents within a therapeutic class may mean that clinicians will be more familiar with these agents and thus, less likely to err.

Automated Dispensing Systems

Automated, point-of-care delivery systems are systems which dispense medications only for patients who should receive them and record what was removed, when, and for what patient. Such systems have many potential benefits including reducing error rates, although these have not always been realized. For example, the rate of errors due to delays in giving patients medications could fall, because of the availability of medications at the point of care. Also, these devices have the potential to decrease the number of missing dose errors.

Although automated distribution systems are attractive, it has not been established that current systems decrease the number of medication errors or even reduce costs. Some early studies, in fact, suggest the opposite: Barker et al[3] found that one such system actually appeared to be associated with an increase in medication errors, and another study found little decrease in time savings with introduction of an automated medication cart filling system.[44] One reason that errors increased with the automated system was that multiple drugs (up to 30) are sometimes put in a single drawer, making it possible to pick the wrong medication. Linking these devices with bar coding should allow the correct medication to be picked; another approach would be to include more, smaller drawers, if practical. Regarding provider time, with effective time-motion studies and human factors engineering, it should be possible to design systems that do save time, particularly with automated filling of carts, which is now available.

Bar Coding

Bar coding of individual medications, patients, and providers is another systems change which might reduce the number of medication errors. Bar coding is inexpensive and has proved to be very effective in other industries, for example, in revolutionizing the way supermarkets maintain inventories. While incorporating bar coding into interventions for reducing medication errors has not received much formal study, bar coding is being used increasingly in other health care areas, such as the clinical laboratory.[45] Currently there is

no standard for bar coding medications, but efforts are underway to push the industry in this direction. In the interim, there are companies that will contract to bar code medications for health care organization. Bar coding has the potential to nearly eliminate drug substitutions by ensuring that the right drug goes to the right patient, and could finally allow health care organizations to know exactly what medications were given, when, and by whom.

Computerized Medication Administration Record

At most health care organizations, the current medication administration record (MAR) is kept on paper, in multiple sheets, and often in places where physicians cannot readily find it. It is often difficult to determine whether and when a medication was given; to find all the antibiotics currently being given, a practitioner might have to go through several pages. Transcription is required to build the record. While nurses do their best to accurately record in the MAR, inaccuracies of a variety of types are frequent. These include inaccurately recording the actual time a medication was given, failure to record doses, especially for as-needed medications, and, less often, inadvertent discontinuation of a medication when MAR sheets are being transcribed. One key issue from the quality perspective is that without adding up doses manually, it is not easy to determine how much of a medication a given patient has received; this is particularly relevant for as-needed medications, such as narcotics, which are often given across several shifts and by nurses who may or may not remember what prior shifts have done. An example is an elderly patient who received 300 mg of meperidine from several different providers over a 12-hour period and eventually became confused, fell from bed, and suffered a fracture.

Computerization of the MAR has a number of advantages. Transcription is eliminated. The record is clear, legible, immediately accessible to all, and can be presented in a variety of views to different providers. Charting is easier, particularly if the system is linked with bar coding. Furthermore, a computerized MAR allows cumulative dose checking and can display a warning to a nurse when a patient has reached his or her "cumulative dose" limit, as in the meperidine example. A potential disadvantage of linking a point-of-care MAR device with bar coding as described above is that it could slow the process. Nurses are extremely busy, and staff-to-patient ratios are being reduced, making it mandatory that the process be made very efficient.

Applications to Specific Care Settings

We have discussed specific strategies to target processes in the medication use system that could decrease medication errors significantly. But which strategies would be best in the different care settings? The following section details which improvements might best be implemented in a given health care organization.

Acute Care

All of the strategies already listed apply in acute care settings. A multidisciplinary panel convened by the American Society of Health-System Pharmacists[1] suggested seven top-priority actions for preventing ADEs in hospitals (Table 4-2, page 67), which can be adapted to other settings as well. The strategy with the greatest long-term potential for preventing medication errors is probably implementation of computerized order entry linked with a role change for pharmacists and targeted physician education. Development of automated dispensing systems, bar coding and computerization of the medication administration record are closely associated, and will be complementary. In the short term, many hospitals will find it easier to use unit dosing, role changes for pharmacists linked with targeted physician education, and computerized pharmacy checking. In both the short and long term, better patient education about medications is also essential.

Long Term Care

Long term care has received comparatively little evaluation, and the issues differ substantially from hospitals, because of the lower acuity, increased number of medications, cognitive impairment, and frailty of most patients. Nurses provide most of the primary care in this setting; physicians and consulting pharmacists often come only once a month. Strategies which are likely to be productive in this setting include nurse education, physician education, changing the role of the pharmacist to allow him or her to become even more proactive, strengthening computerized pharmacy checking (already in place for many nursing homes), and putting in place computerized physician order entry. Physician order entry could have an especially large impact, since many errors appear to be made by covering physicians who have relatively little patient information available to them at the time of order writing. Having a computerized electronic record could substantially improve matters.

Many other problems stem from failure to recognize drug-related complications or to communicate them to physicians in ways that result in action. Early data from a large study on medication problems in long term care[53] suggest that there are many instances in which nursing did not recognize the relationship between a drug and a side effect, did note it but didn't contact the physician, or attempted to contact the physician but was unable to get the physician to change therapy. Educating nurses to recognize these problems and

Table 4-2. Top-Priority Actions for Preventing Adverse Drug Events

1. Establish processes in which prescribers enter medication orders directly into computer systems.

2. Evaluate the use of machine-readable coding (eg, bar coding) in medication-use processes.

3. Develop better systems for monitoring and reporting adverse drug events.

4. Use unit dose–medication distribution and pharmacy-based intravenous admixture systems.

5. Assign pharmacists to work in patient care areas in direct collaboration with prescribers and those administering medications.

6. Approach medication errors as systems failures and seek systems solutions to preventing them.

7. Ensure that medication orders are routinely reviewed by a pharmacist before first doses and ensure that prescribers, pharmacists, nurses and other workers seek resolution whenever there is any question of safety with respect to medication use.

Source: Adapted from American Society for Health-System Pharmacists: ASHP's Guidelines on Preventing Medication Errors in Hospitals. *Am J Hosp Pharm* 50:305–14, 1993.

to communicate effectively with physicians about problems could have a significant impact on preventing errors in long term care settings.

Home Care
Although Medicare expenditures for home health care are growing exponentially, the available data suggest that home health care is not replacing acute care or preventing admissions in the Medicare program, as was originally intended.[54] Moreover, the home care providers do not have ready access to hospital or clinic information. This is particularly problematic with medication use. It is common for the patient to be taking one set of medications at home, then to be discharged after hospitalization with a different set of medications, and have the primary care provider believe he or she is taking a third set. Improving the communication links between the involved parties is essential. Beyond improving communication, key strategies in this area include targeted provider education (primarily for the nurses who are following patients), computerization of the record

including medication ordering, standardization of processes, and development of patient-centered prevention strategies.

Ambulatory Care
This is another area which has received comparatively little attention, and is thus fertile ground for medication use system improvements. Clearly, patient-centered strategies will play the largest role, including developing better materials and making information available in new ways, perhaps over the Internet and via call-in centers. Computerized order entry should have a very large impact in acute care as well, and direct transmission of electronic orders to pharmacies could eliminate most of the many errors associated with handwritten prescriptions. Legislation is currently pending in many areas to make this possible. In the interim, computerized pharmacy checking is employed by many commercial pharmacies, but the primary shortcoming has been that they have relatively little in the way of clinical data, so that to date they perform mostly

drug-drug and drug-allergy checking. Such checking would be better done using the patient's medical record at the time of prescribing, because patients may get medications from multiple pharmacies and physicians, and any individual pharmacy may not have an up-to-date profile for a specific patient.

Systems for Monitoring Medication Error and ADE Frequency

Systems for monitoring are an important adjunct to improving care in this area. In quality improvement in general, it is useful to have quality measures which can be tracked over time and can provide both rates and "critical incidents." For ADEs and medication errors, most quality measurement in health care organizations has relied on the incident reporting system, which identifies only about 1 in 20 ADEs,[46] and likely an even lower proportion of medication errors. It may thus be effective for providing critical incidents, but cannot give reliable data about ADE rates.

For ADE detection, the main methods have been chart review, stimulated voluntary reporting, and computerized monitoring, in which a program searches the computerized medical record routinely to look for signals suggesting the presence of an ADE such as the use of an antidote or a new allergy, which can then be followed up by a pharmacist. In a direct comparison of these methods, chart review identified 65%; of all ADEs voluntary reporting identified 4%; and computerized monitoring identified 45%.[47] The types of events identified varied by method.

Though chart review is an effective method for detecting ADEs, its expense makes it impractical for ongoing quality monitoring in most health care organizations;[47] use of computerized monitoring is much less expensive. Classen et al[18] developed an ADE monitor at LDS Hospital in Salt Lake City, Utah, and found mainly moderate to severe ADEs that occurred in 2% of all admissions. If such an approach is in place, combined with simplified spontaneous voluntary reporting, the same pharmacist who follows up computer-generated signals suggesting the presence of ADEs can follow up spontaneous reports. These computer monitors, however, are still not widely used,[48] the main barriers being, perhaps, the lack of an "off-the-shelf" commercial product and the resource commitment to a quality-oriented clinical pharmacist. Nonetheless, this approach probably does represent the strategy of the future.

A more difficult issue is how to routinely measure medication errors (in order to ascertain total ADEs).[6] Because of the high number, it would be too expensive to measure them all. A more practical approach may be to perform targeted intensive collection according to the systems changes being implemented. For example, in an administration intervention, a direct observation approach would be effective, while in an ordering intervention a strategy involving routine order review would be more effective. For routine data collection, voluntary reporting may still be useful to turn up errors which can be used in a critical incident approach.

Adopting a Multidisciplinary Systems Approach

A key to error prevention, as noted earlier, is changing the organization perspective about errors. Such change will take several years in most organizations, but without it, major improvement will be difficult. There are two main roadblocks in current organization cultures: a tendency to blame individuals and the "silo effect." The issues surrounding blame of individuals for errors have been discussed earlier (see page 53). The silo effect is the tendency in an improvement project for each of the groups involved to focus largely on only its own piece of the process.

In the inpatient setting, the key groups involved in the medication use system are physicians, nurses and pharmacists, who all tend to stay within their own silo. In many settings there may be significant antagonism, particularly between nursing and pharmacy. For example, pharmacists may believe that nursing is to blame for missing dose errors while nurses feel that medications don't arrive in a timely fashion from the pharmacy. The nurses compensate by developing floor stocks or borrowing from other patients when a medication is not immediately available. Physicians may simply want to get their work done, and at times be resentful when called about problems with their orders. Overall, there may be acrimony among the groups, with each believing that another is "the problem."

To make meaningful changes in the medication process, all of the above groups need to work together as a team. Often, a change that makes sense from one group's perspective (for example, eliminating the pharmacy hot-line for calls about medication questions to eliminate a pharmacy full-time employee) may be counterproductive when viewed from the organization perspective. A multidisciplinary group, involving each discipline, is much more likely to make effective changes than, for example, the pharmacy director acting alone. The pharmacy and therapeutics (P&T) committee can play a key role in this regard, but actual process changes would probably be better handled by small subgroups authorized by the P&T committee because of the unwieldiness of making changes through large committees. The P&T committee should include representatives of nursing, pharmacy, key physician groups, and any other appropriate staff, such as administration. Furthermore, this group should ideally use data from a system which routinely monitors medication errors and other ADEs, so that it can have some idea about how to prioritize.

An illustrative example is the former system for handling allergies at Brigham and Women's Hospital in Boston. As at other hospitals, the medication use systems were never consciously designed, but just "grew up."[20] Allergies were recorded in patient care notes by a variety of practitioners, including medical students, physicians, and nurses. Physicians were supposed to write allergies in the admitting orders, although in practice this did not always occur and these notations rarely included what reaction was expected. Unit clerks were supposed to write allergies at the top of every order sheet, although in practice this was rarely done, and even when it was done, providers often ignored it (there are examples of orders in which an allergy is recorded at the top of the page with an order for the medication lower down). Pharmacists relied on the order sheets sent from the physicians to record allergies, and because of their workload, it was rarely practical for pharmacists to contact the patient themselves. Detection for known allergies was done by pharmacist inspection, by comparing the medication ordered and the list of known allergies. Allergies noted in the outpatient clinic or those noted in previous admissions were not carried forward. Not surprisingly, a significant proportion of allergy errors slipped through. This approach is probably typical of those in place in many health care organizations today.

In contrast, the current computerized allergy detection system now in place at Brigham and Women's Hospital requires allergies and the specific reaction to be entered by practitioners at admission. If no allergies are entered, the practitioner is prompted to enter them at 24 hours and at subsequent intervals. The allergy list, including those from prior visits and the ambulatory care setting, is kept in one place, and allergy detection processes use drug families such as penicillins and cephalosporins. Detection is not by inspection but automated, using direct electronic matching between the drugs ordered and the computerized allergy list, so that 100% of allergies detected are reported to the prescriber upon order entry and, if the prescriber chooses to override, to the pharmacist, who decides whether additional discussion with the prescriber is needed. This is an example of a forcing function:[27] the clinician cannot write an order for a patient with a known allergy without making a conscious choice to do so. An example of this from the automotive industry is the design feature that will not allow a car to be put into reverse unless one foot is on the brake. Occasional instances involving allergies still arise when the provider overrides inappropriately, and pharmacy review is a very valuable safety net.

Another important systems issue is the need for communication among different information systems within an organization, such as the pharmacy and laboratory systems.[33] Clinicians often need to know a specific laboratory test when ordering a given medication (for example, the potassium level when ordering furosemide). At Brigham and Women's Hospital, they try to anticipate these needs and display such information in the computerized patient record.[33,41]

Patient-Centered Prevention Strategies

Patient-centered approaches, including patient education materials and counseling, are particularly important in ambulatory care settings and at the time of discharge from any health care organization. As patients are discharged "quicker and sicker" from the acute care setting, the transition from discharge to the patient's return home is particularly intense. In one study evaluating this transition, Johnson evaluated 335 prescriptions for 192 pediatric patients being discharged from the hospital.[49] Differences among the prescriptions, discharge instruction sheets, and medication labels

were found for 12% of the medications prescribed at discharge. Also, only 44% of families received counseling about proper medication administration by their pharmacists. In a study evaluating the effectiveness of patient information, a trial showed that the percent of errors was reduced about 3-fold by giving out leaflets about the involved medications, and that "easy" leaflets had a much greater impact than "moderate" or "hard" leaflets.[50] In another study evaluating how the transition from inpatient to ambulatory care could be handled better, Sands developed and evaluated a computer program designed to improve the discharge process by providing guidance to the physicians in writing the discharge prescriptions, offering educational material to patients, and notifying primary care physicians about medication changes.[51] Although this program was well received by patients, nurses, and physicians, there was no difference in length of stay, time to emergency readmission, or number of medications prescribed between the intervention and control groups, although there was a nonsignificant trend toward better compliance in the intervention group. In another study aimed at reducing medication errors in a geriatric population, Martin and Mead found that the combination of color-coded bottles and a color-coded weekly pill tray resulted in the smallest deviation from the ideal pill count, 1.7% versus 17.1% for controls.[52] More data are needed about how to improve the transition from hospital to home, and about the effectiveness of approaches for reducing the likelihood of medication errors for ambulatory care patients.

Medication Error Prevention: The Future

What does the future hold for the medication use system? The medication system of the future will be much more effective at preventing errors and more efficient in general; it will clearly include much more automation and more checks and balances.[55] Providers will use order-entry systems for both inpatients and outpatients. These systems will make a variety of suggestions to providers at the time of ordering, displaying appropriate doses and guidelines, and, in the background, checking for problems such as allergies and interactions. In complex situations, specifically those in which the physician is not already convinced about the suggestion being made, face-to-face counter-detailing will be used.

Orders will be transmitted directly to the pharmacy, which will perform additional checks. They will be electronically triaged according to urgency and whether they can be obtained from a point-of-care distribution system, or need to be prepared and delivered by the pharmacy. The medications already present at the point-of-care will be made immediately available using an automated distribution system. When nurses give medications, they will take the drug from the drawer, check it with a bar code reader to document that they have taken the correct medication, and then give it to the patient, after "wanding" the bar code on both their own and the patient's identification bracelet to ensure that the medication is intended for the particular patient. Bar coding will minimize the chance of several problems: giving one patient another's drug, giving medications too early, and "look-alike" substitu-

tions. It will also "close the loop" of drug administration, making it possible to determine how much drug has been given, when, and to whom.[55]

Patients and caregivers will receive education both during the hospitalization and at discharge, and will get printouts of information detailing how their medications should be taken and discussing side effects. This and other information will also be available to them at home over the Internet or through the home care nurse following them. The home care nurse will be able to access the electronic medical record from the patient's home, facilitating communication about the intended plan and the patient's response. Practitioners will be able to write electronic prescriptions which can be sent directly to outpatient pharmacies.

Quality will be monitored using computerized detection systems and a voluntary system parallel to the incident reporting system to allow detection of near misses; in both instances, pharmacists will follow up individual incidents. A multidisciplinary group charged with improving the system will recommend periodic changes and updates based on this information.

The next chapter is a workbook section to help your organization work towards this vision of the medication use system of the future.

References

1. ASHP guidelines on preventing medication errors in hospitals. *Am J Hosp Pharm* 50:305–314, 1993.

2. Allan EL, Barker KN: Fundamentals of medication error research. *Am J Hosp Pharm* 47:555–571, 1993.

3. Barker KN, Allan EL: Research on drug-use-system errors. *Am J Health Syst Pharm* 52:400–403, 1995.

4. Lesar TS, Briceland LL, Delcoure K, et al: Medication prescribing errors in a teaching hospital. *JAMA* 263:2329–2334, 1990.

5. Folli HL, Poole RL, Benitz WE, Russo JC: Medication error prevention by clinical pharmacists in two children's hospitals. *Pediatrics* 79:718–722, 1987.

6. Bates DW, Boyle DL, Vander Vliet MB, Schneider J, Leape LL: Relationship between medication errors and adverse drug events. *J Gen Intern Med* 10:199–205, 1995.

7. Van Leeuwen DH: Are medication error rates useful as comparative measures of organizational performance? *Jt Comm J Qual Improv* 20:192–199, 1994.

8. Classen DC, Pestotnik SL, Evans RS, Burke JP: Computerized surveillance of adverse drug events in hospital patients. *JAMA* 266:2847–2851, 1991.

9. Faich GA: National adverse drug reaction reporting. 1984–1989. *Arch Intern Med* 151:1645–1647, 1991.

10. Faich GA: Adverse-drug-reaction monitoring. *N Engl J Med* 314:1589–1592, 1986.

11. Melmon KL: Preventable drug reactions—Causes and cures. *N Engl J Med* 284:1361–1367, 1971.

12. Keith MR, Bellanger-McCleery RA, Fuchs JE Jr: Multidisciplinary program for detecting and evaluating adverse drug reactions. *Am J Hosp Pharm* 46:1809–1812, 1989.

13. Seidl LG, Thornton G, Smith JW, et al: Studies on the epidemiology of adverse drug reactions: III. Reactions in patients on a general medical service. *Bull Hosp Johns Hopkins Hosp* 119:299–315, 1966.

14. Jick H: Adverse drug reactions: The magnitude of the problem. *J Allergy Clin Immunol* 74:555–557, 1984.

15. Hoddinott BC, Gowdey CW, Coulter WK, et al: Drug reactions and errors in administration on a medical ward. *Can Med Assoc J* 97:1001–1006, 1967.

16. Ogilvie RI, Ruedy J: Adverse drug reactions during hospitalization. *Can Med Assoc J* 97:1450–1457, 1967.

17. Hurwitz N, Wade OL: Intensive hospital monitoring of adverse reactions to drugs. *Br Med J* 1:531–536, 1969.

18. Berry LL, Segal R, Sherrin TP, Fudge KA: Sensitivity and specificity of three methods of detecting adverse drug reactions. *Am J Hosp Pharm* 45:1534–1539, 1988.

19. Karch FE, Lasagna L: Adverse drug reactions: A critical review. *JAMA* 234:1236–1241, 1975.

20. Bates DW, Cullen D, Laird N, et al: Incidence of adverse drug events and potential adverse drug events: Implications for prevention. *JAMA* 274:29–34, 1995.

21. Leape LL, Bates DW, Cullen DJ, et al: Systems analysis of adverse drug events. *JAMA* 274:35–43, 1995.

22. Johnson JA, Bootman JL: Drug-related morbidity and mortality: A cost-of-illness model. *Arch Intern Med* 155:1949–1956, 1995.

23. Deming WE: *Out of the Crisis.* Cambridge, MA: MIT-CAES, 1986.

24. Juran JM: *Quality Control Handbook.* New York: McGraw Hill, 1988.

25. Berwick DM: Continuous improvement as an ideal in health care. *New Engl J Med* 320:53–56, 1989.

26. Laffel G, Blumenthal D: The case for using industrial quality management science in health care organizations. *JAMA* 262:2869–2873, 1989.

27. Leape LL: Error in medicine. *JAMA* 272:1851–1857, 1995.

28. National Coordinating Council for Medication Error Reporting and Prevention: Council identifies and makes recommendations to improve error-prone aspects of prescription writing. Press Release 96C03. Rockville, MD: U.S. Pharmacopeia, September 4, 1996.

29. Shultz SM, White SJ, Latiolais CJ: Medication errors reduced by unit-dose. *Hospitals* 47:106–112, 1973.

30. Simborg DW, Derewicz HJ: A highly automated hospital medication system. Five years' experience and evaluation. *Ann Intern Med* 83:342–346, 1975.

31. Soumerai SB, Avorn J: Efficacy and cost-containment in hospital pharmacotherapy: State of the art and future directions. *Milbank Mem Fund Q Health Soc* 62:447–474, 1984.

32. Ambrose PJ, Smith WE, Palarea ER: A decade of experience with a clinical pharmacokinetics service. *Am J Hosp Pharm* 45:1879–1886, 1988.

33. Bates DW, Kuperman G, Teich JM: Computerized physician order entry and quality of care. *Qual Manag Health Care* 2(4):18–27, 1994.

34. Brown G: Assessing the clinical impact of pharmacists' interventions. *Am J Hosp Pharm* 48:2644–2647, 1991.

35. Hawkey CJ, Hodgson S, Norman A, Daneshmend TK, Garner ST: Effect of reactive pharmacy intervention on quality of hospital prescribing. *Br Med J* 300:986–990, 1990.

36. Blum KV, Abel SR, Urbanski CJ, Pierce JM: Medication error prevention by pharmacists. *Am J Hosp Pharm* 45:1902–1903, 1988.

37. Shulman JI, Shulman S, Haines AP: The prevention of adverse drug reactions—A potential role for pharmacists in the primary care team? *J R Coll Gen Pract* 31:429–434, 1981.

38. Bond CA, Raehl CL, Pitterle ME: 1992 National Clinical Pharmacy Services study. *Pharmacotherapy* 14:282–304, 1994.

39. Cavuto NJ, Woosley RL, Sale M: Pharmacies and prevention of potentially fatal drug interactions. *JAMA* 275:1086–1087, 1996.

40. Sittig DF, Stead WW: Computer-based physician order entry: The state of the art. *J Am Med Inform Assoc* 1:108–123, 1994.

41. Tierney WM, Miller ME, Overhage JM, McDonald CJ: Physician inpatient order writing on microcomputer workstations. Effects on resource utilization. *JAMA* 269:379–383, 1993.

42. Raschke RA, Reilly BM, Guidry JR, Fontana JR, Srinivas S: The weight-based heparin nomogram compared with a "standard care" nomogram. *Ann Intern Med* 119:874–881, 1993.

43. Bates DW, O'Neil AC, Boyle D, et al: Potential identifiability and preventability of adverse events using information systems. *J Am Med Inform Assoc* 1:404–411, 1994.

44. Klein EG, Santora JA, Pascale PM, Kitrenos JG: Medication cart-filling time, accuracy and cost with an automated dispensing system. *Am J Hosp Pharm* 51:1193–1196, 1994.

45. Brient K: Barcoding facilitates patient-focused care. *Healthc Inform* 12:38, 40, 42, 1995.

46. Cullen DJ, Bates DW, Small SD, Cooper JB, Nemeskal AR, Leape LL: The incident reporting system does not detect adverse drug events: A problem for quality improvement. *Jt Comm J Qual Improv* 21:541–548, 1995.

47. Jha AK, Kuperman GJ, Teich JM, et al: Adverse drug events: Development of a computer-based monitor and comparison with chart review and stimulated voluntary report. *J Am Med Inform Assoc* 5:305–314, 1998.

48. Koch KE: Use of standardized screening procedures to identify adverse drug reactions. *Am J Hosp Pharm* 47:1314–1320, 1990.

49. Johnson KB, Butta JK, Donohue PK, Glenn DJ, Holtzman NA: Discharging patients with prescriptions instead of medications: Sequelae in a teaching hospital. *Pediatrics* 97:481–485, 1996.

50. Ley P, Jain VK, Skilbeck CE: A method for decreasing patients' medication errors. *Psychol Med* 6:599–601, 1976.

51. Sands DZ, Safran C: Closing the loop of patient care— A clinical trial of a computerized discharge medication program. *Proc Annu Symp Comput Appl Med Care* 841–845, 1994.

52. Martin DC, Mead K: Reducing medication errors in a geriatric population. *J Am Ger Soc* 30(4):258–260, 1982.

53. Gurwitz JH, Sanchez-Cross MT, Eckler MA, Matulis J: The epidemiology of adverse and unexpected events in the long-term care setting. *J Am Ger Soc* 42:33–38, 1994.

54. Welch HG, Wennberg DE, Welch WP: The use of Medicare home health care services. *New Engl J Med* 335:324–329, 1996.

55. Bates DW: Medication errors. How common are they and what can be done to prevent them? *Drug Saf* 5:303–310, 1996.

56. U.S. Pharmacopeia: *USP DI Drug Information for the Health Care Professional*. Rockville, MD: U.S. Pharmacopeial Convention, 1998.

Chapter 5

EVALUATING AND IMPROVING YOUR MEDICATION USE SYSTEM

Linda S Hanold, MHSA
Deputy Director, Department of Research and Evaluation
Joint Commission on Accreditation of Healthcare Organizations
Oakbrook Terrace, Illinois

Bruce E Vinson, PharmD
Administrative Director for Pharmacy Services
Baptist Memorial Hospital
Memphis, Tennessee

Annette Rubino, MBA, CPhT
Performance Measurement Manager
Joint Commission on Accreditation of Healthcare Organizations
Oakbrook Terrace, Illinois

This chapter is designed to guide you through the steps of designing and implementing a performance improvement project for your medication use system. Each section addresses a step in the process and gives you a list of activities to be performed or questions to be answered. At the end of each section, you will find explanations and examples of the performance improvement tools you will be using in that section, along with easy-to-follow instructions in the "Tools to Use" area.

You can use this chapter to identify and undertake a medication use process improvement activity, or you can customize components (activities and tools) to be consistent with whatever improvement approach your organization uses. Let creativity be your guide and adapt this chapter to meet your unique performance measurement and improvement needs. Chapter 6 presents a case study which puts the working principles outline in this chapter to use in an actual organization.

Approaches to Improvement

The basic process outlined in this chapter is a hybrid of well-known performance improvement methods, including the plan-do-study-act (PDSA) cycle, the FOCUS plan-do-check-act (FOCUS-PDCA) cycle, and the Institute for Healthcare Improvement's rapid cycle improvement (RCI). Before beginning, you may find it helpful to review the basic tenets of these methods.

The most famous is the PDSA cycle, which is also called the PDCA (substituting check for study) or the Shewhart cycle. In this cycle,

- *plan* refers to first understanding the process, then proposing an action aimed at improvement, and finally deciding how the action will be tested and how data will be collected to determine what effect the action has;

- *do* is performing the test by implementing the action on a small scale;

- *study* involves analyzing the effect of the action being tested; and

- *act* means to fully implement the action or reassess the improvement action taken and perhaps choose another action.

The cycle is continuous and can be entered at any point.

The FOCUS-PDCA model was developed by the Hospital Corporation of America (now part of Columbia Health Care Corporation). In this approach, FOCUS stands for:

- Find a process to improve;

- Organize a team that knows the process;

- Clarify current knowledge of the process;

- Understand causes of process variation; and

- Select the process improvement.

The PDCA cycle is then used to test and implement the process improvement.

Rapid cycle improvement (RCI) was developed by the Institute for Healthcare Improvement and has been used successfully to improve processes in many areas, including reducing adverse drug events (ADEs) and medication errors, cesarean section rates, delays in waiting times, and costs, as well as improving outcomes in adult intensive care. This method depends on a very aggressive approach to process improvement. The model for improvement focuses on three fundamental questions:

- What are we trying to accomplish?

- How will we know that a "change" is an improvement?

- What changes can we make that will result in an improvement?

This method is primarily dependent on stringing multiple PDSA cycles together with rapid turnover of each cycle building upon the last. In RCI, areas for improvement are identified anecdotally (hunches, theories, or ideas), improvements are implemented on a small scale, and results are measured. Positive results lead to broader implementation of the improvement and serve as the basis for the next PDSA cycle. Each cycle can be accomplished in as little as two weeks, depending on the nature of the improvement being studied.

Preparing for Performance Improvement

Before you can begin the actual process of planning, designing, and implementing your performance improvement project, you must lay the foundation. To improve a system or process, you must

- work with the people involved,

- know the system's or process's goals, and

- thoroughly understand all the steps involved.

Organize a Performance Improvement Team

Identify individuals across your organization who are familiar with the medication use system in your organization. Identify those who can be most instrumental in recognizing areas for potential improvement and implementing those improvements. Your process improvement team should span all staff levels, departments, and disciplines, and it should include appropriate leadership involvement. List the members of your performance improvement team and their titles here.

Team Member Name

Team Member Title

_____   _____

_____   _____

_____   _____

_____   _____

_____   _____

_____   _____

_____   _____

Identify the Goals of the Medication Use System

A system should be designed or redesigned with a particular purpose(s) in mind, because the outcome of any system is directly dependent on its fundamental design. Thus, if the design of the system is altered, the outcomes will be affected proportionately. If your organization is experiencing five medication use errors per week, your medication use system may be perfectly designed to yield five medication errors per week.

Reducing medication errors in your organization begins with the performance improvement team articulating, evaluating, and perhaps redesigning your medication use system. Begin by defining the goals of your organization's ideal medication use system (for example, to maintain costs, to provide high-quality patient care, to interact effectively with other health care professionals, to minimize the risk of medication error). List them in the space provided.

1. _____

2. _____

3. _____

4. _____

Develop a Flowchart of Your Medication Use System

A clear understanding of your system is essential before plans can be formulated. Clarify your organization's current medication use system by developing a flowchart, using the instructions in the "Tools to Use" section (page 80). The flowchart will help team members see how the process actually works, which is often quite different from how they think it works or should work. You may want to create a separate flowchart that represents the ideal path of the process, and then compare the two charts for discrepancies.

As you analyze the steps in your flowchart, identify and list potentially vulnerable areas where errors may be introduced.

1. _____

2. _____

3. _____

4. _____

5. _____

6. _____

Organize and Apply Current Knowledge

Organize current information about known medication errors in your organization into the table provided and crosswalk each occurrence to a point in your medication use system flowchart. Consider a defined period of time (for example, one year, one quarter) when listing known medication errors. Column labels should be customized to capture the information you believe to be most relevant to your decision-making process (for example, "number of occurrences" may not be a useful column if each medication error has a different level of severity, cost, and/or flowchart reference associated with it).

Types of Known Medication Errors	Number of Occurrences	Severity of Occurrence(s)	Other Considerations (outcome, cost, etc)	Source of Error (if known)	Flowchart Reference
Medication Overdose	3	Moderate—required antidote	No harm/cost of antidote ($7.82)	Wrong dose was prescribed	Prescribing

Next, analyze the distribution of known medication errors across your medication use system. Identify those points that appear to be most vulnerable to error. List and rank order identified flowchart components in order of most to least number of associated errors. Put an asterisk (*) beside those where errors resulted in severe consequences (for example, permanent harm, death, resuscitation, extraordinary costs).

Medication Use Process Component   Number of Occurrences at this Process Point

_____   _____

_____   _____

_____   _____

_____   _____

Compare the flowchart components identified in your analysis (page 78) and those identified in the preceding step. List those components which appear in both lists.

1. _____

2. _____

3. _____

4. _____

Tools to Use

Flowcharts. A flowchart is a graphic representation of a process. It is designed to help teams understand all the steps in a process or system using common, easily recognized symbols. Flowcharts help identify inefficiencies, misunderstandings, redundancies, and areas of neglect, while providing insight into how a given process should be performed. They show a clear picture of the process and provide the people involved at the various steps with an understanding of the whole. The following steps will guide you in developing your own flowchart:

1. *Decide on starting and ending points of the process.* This step helps contain the chart within manageable boundaries. The team may change the boundaries later if the process proves to be several processes in one.

2. *Brainstorm and record all activities and decision points in the process.* Look for specific activities and decisions necessary to keep the process moving to its conclusion. This should be done by those most familiar with the various parts of the process, with assistance as necessary from people outside the team.

3. *Arrange the activities and decision points in sequence.* Some activities may appear to occur simultaneously, while others may seem disconnected; certain decisions may cause steps to be repeated.

4. *Use this information to create the flowchart.* Place each activity in a box and place each decision point in a diamond (see Figure 5-1, page 81). Connect these with lines and arrows to indicate the flow of the process.

5. *Analyze the flowchart.* Look for redundancies, inefficiencies, misunderstandings, and any other difficulties. Make sure that every feedback loop has an escape. Make the chart your basis for designing an improved process, using spots where the process works well as models for improvement.

Brainstorming. Brainstorming can be used any time a team needs multiple ideas or a fresh perspective. It can be used at any stage of the performance improvement process, including planning, determining what processes to measure, determining what data to collect, interpreting data, and identifying potential improvement actions. The five steps of brainstorming start on page 82.

Sample Flowchart: Medication Administration

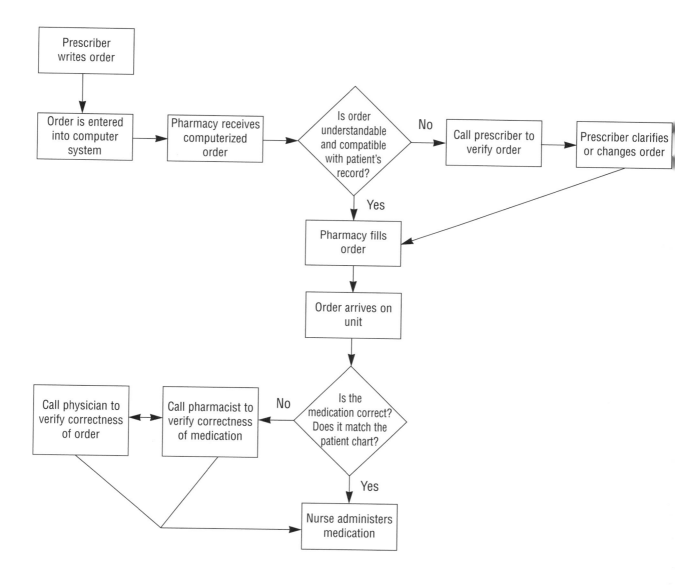

Figure 5-1. *This flowchart shows the basic steps in a traditional medication use system. The process components are arranged sequentially, and each stage can be expanded as necessary to show all possible steps.*

1. *Define the subject.* This ensures that your session will have direction. The group should be told up front that any idea is welcome, no matter how broad or narrow in scope, how serious or bizarre in nature. All ideas are valuable in a brainstorming session, as long as they address the subject at hand.

2. *Think briefly about the issue.* Allow enough time for team members to gather their thoughts, but not enough time for detailed analysis. Group members should not have time to second-guess their ideas; this stifles creative thought.

3. *Set a time limit.* Agree on a time limit for the brainstorming session. Depending on the size of the group, 10 to 20 minutes should be adequate.

4. *Generate ideas.* This part of the brainstorming process can follow a structured or an unstructured format. In the structured format, group members express ideas by taking turns in a predetermined order; the process continues in rotation until either time runs out or ideas are exhausted. This method encourages participation by every member, but may result in a more pressured atmosphere. In the unstructured format, group members voice ideas as they come to mind. This method is more relaxed, but the facilitator must be sure that the more vocal members of the group do not dominate the session.

   Regardless of the format, it is crucial that neither the leader nor the other group members comment on any given idea. Reactions of any kind are inhibiting at this stage and can undermine the process. Be sure to write down every idea.

5. *Clarify ideas.* In this final step, the goal is to make sure that all ideas are recorded accurately and are understood by the group. There should be no attempt yet to rank or otherwise judge the ideas. Multivoting, described next in this section, will help with that task.

Multivoting. Multivoting is a technique for narrowing a broad list of ideas down to those that are most important. Using this technique, members of a team work together to determine which are the few critical ideas worthy of immediate attention.

Multivoting requires a predetermined list of ideas and a designated team member to guide the group through the following process:

1. *Combine any items that are the same or similar.* Almost any list will have some overlap, so ask the team whether similar items can be grouped together. The key is *asking*. Faith in the process will be damaged if members feel that their ideas are being altered without permission.

2. *Number the items on the new list.* Numbering helps the team refer to specific items readily.

3. *Determine the number of points that will be assigned to the list by each group member.* Each member uses points to vote on different items on the list. A typical number of points would be between 5 and 10. An easy way to determine the number of points each member will distribute is to divide the total number of items on the list by 4. For example, if there are 20 items, each member would have 5 points to distribute.

4. *Allow time for group members to independently assign points.* Members are allowed to distribute points any way they want.

5. *Indicate each member's point allocation on the list.* Gather each member's votes and mark those votes on the list next to each item.

6. *Tally the votes.* Write the total for each item so that the team can see the results.

7. *Note items with the greatest number of points.* Often one or more ideas will be the obvious favorites; sometimes a clear second and third choice will emerge. Occasionally, the votes will be evenly distributed with no clear preferences.

8. *Choose the final group or multivote again.* If a group of items is clearly the team's preference, this group is considered the final list. If points are too evenly distributed, the team may multivote again, leaving out the two or three lowest items or reducing the number of points each member can assign.

Planning the Performance Improvement Project

Using the information you gathered in the preceding section, you can begin to plan what processes in your medication system need to be addressed and how you will address them.

Targeting/Selecting Areas for Improvement

All areas identified through the flowchart analysis (page 78) and the organizing and clarifying current knowledge exercise (page 79) are important areas to target for improvement. However, those identified as being common to both levels of analysis (page 80) may be the ones on which you want to focus your initial improvement efforts. Depending on the team's assessment, other areas may be identified as having greater priority based on overriding criteria (for example, those areas where a significant number of errors have occurred or those areas where there have been extremely severe consequences). Therefore, as a final check, generate a list of all areas identified in the flowchart analysis and the organizing and clarifying current knowledge exercise for potential improvement, indicating their priority as high, medium, or low. (See "Tools to Use" section on pages 86–87 for ways to prioritize areas for improvement.)

Potential Area for Improvement   **Priority**

_____   _____

_____   _____

_____   _____

_____   _____

_____   _____

1. Consider the areas that have been identified as high priority and define the targeted improvement (for example, to implement improvements that will affect physician prescribing behaviors).

Area for Improvement   **Targeted Improvement**

_____   _____

_____   _____

_____   _____

_____   _____

_____   _____

Is each targeted improvement under the control or within the purview of the team or your health care organization? (For example, increasing knowledge of pharmacy staff is a reasonable objective, but may not be under the control of your organization if you work with an outside pharmacy.)

____yes ____no

2. Verify that these areas are in need of improvement through additional (concurrent or retrospective) data collection, if needed. Is your current information sufficient and reliable? (For example, is the data relative to prescribing errors accurate and complete.)

____yes ____no

If additional data are needed to substantiate the need for improvement in these areas, what kind and how many data will be needed? Be specific in your answer. For example, the data currently on hand may be relatively "old" data, so the team recommends a retrospective review of all inpatient physician orders for the most recent quarter to determine whether the incidence of error or need for intervention resulting from wrong-dose orders continues to be a pervasive problem.

_____

_____

_____

_____

_____

_____

Define how the data will be collected.

_____

_____

_____

_____

_____

Who will be responsible for collecting, summarizing, interpreting, and presenting the additional data?

Team Member Name	Team Member Title
_____	_____
_____	_____
_____	_____
_____	_____

3. Conduct a literature review. Don't reinvent the wheel! Search existing literature to determine what work has already been done in the area you are planning to improve. Build on that body of work. List articles resulting from your literature search that are directly relevant to your performance improvement initiative. Note key points from relevant articles. Provide copies of these articles to all team members.

Reference	Key Points
_____	_____
_____	_____
_____	_____
_____	_____

4. Clarify the goals of the identified improvement. Once the area for improvement has been defined and the need for improvement verified, clarify the goals of improvement (for example, prevention/reduction of medication errors, cost savings, expense reduction, redistribution of staff, justification for additional staff). List the goals for your identified improvement initiative.

a. _____

b. _____

c. _____

d. _____

e. _____

Discover the Root Causes of Identified Areas

Select the areas the team has rated top priority and develop cause-and-effect diagrams for each to determine the root causes of the problems (use the instructions under "Tools to Use," pages 87–88). A detailed cause-and-effect diagram can help the team identify specific changes necessary for improvement.

Tools to Use

Selection grids. Selection grids are tools used to help a team select a single option out of several possibilities. They involve setting important criteria that are used as a basis for reaching a decision acceptable to the group. The following steps are used to create a selection grid:

1. *Start with a list of options.* The list should be limited at the outset. More than eight options will complicate the grid and the selection process.

2. *Choose criteria and a scoring system.* No more than four or five criteria, stated in either positive or negative terms, should be used; they may be acquired by brainstorming and multivoting. Once the criteria are defined, a scoring system must be established. The team may choose a simple yes/no system to indicate whether a criterion is met, or adopt a more sophisticated scoring system.

3. *Draw the grid.* List criteria across the top of a page and options down the left side, and then draw a grid so that there is a box (cell) to represent each possible combination of criteria and options. A final column should be included at the right edge to show the total score for each option. Figure 5-2 (page 87) shows an example.

4. *Judge each option against the criteria and write in the scores.* This step should be completed by the team as a whole, facilitated by the leader, and displayed for all to see.

5. *Use the completed grid to evaluate findings.* Ask the following questions: Does one or more option clearly meet all the criteria? Have any options been clearly eliminated? If an option meets most but not all of the criteria, is it still worth considering?

Sample Selection Grid: Improvement Priorities

Process Stage \ Decision Factor	Quality of Care	Patient Satisfaction	Training Resources	Risk Management	Cost Control	Total
Computer order-entry errors						
Pharmacist checks off all orders against patient records						
Multidisciplinary selection of best drug therapy regimen						
Timely delivery of medication						
Patient education for self-administration						

Scoring Key: 3 = strong effect; 2 = some effect; 1 = weak effect; 0 = no effect

Figure 5–2. *This figure shows a selection grid that could be used to set priorities for improvement among process stages where medication errors have occurred. Scores can be assigned to indicate how strongly each decision factor is counted for each improvement opportunity. Once the scores are totaled, they should indicate the overall priority of improvement activities.*

6. *Determine whether new criteria, or adjustments to existing criteria, are necessary.* If all or most of the options meet most or all of the criteria, some change in the criteria may be necessary.

7. *Select the best option.* Using the scoring system, select the option or options that best fulfill the criteria.

Cause-and-effect diagrams. Cause-and-effect diagrams are particularly helpful in the improvement process because they present a clear picture of the many causal relationships between outcomes and the factors in those outcomes. The following steps will help you create a cause-and-effect diagram.

1. *Identify the outcome or problem statement.* This statement defines the effect for which the team will identify possible causes; in this case, the problem statement is one of the areas that have been identified as high priority areas for improvement in the preceding exercise. Place it on the right side of the page, halfway down, and then draw an arrow horizontally across the page, pointing to the outcome (for example, physician prescribing behaviors).

2. *Determine general categories for the causes.* Common categories include work methods, personnel, materials, and equipment. Represent these on the diagram by connecting them with diagonal lines branch-

Sample Cause-and-Effect Diagram: Wrong-Dose Error

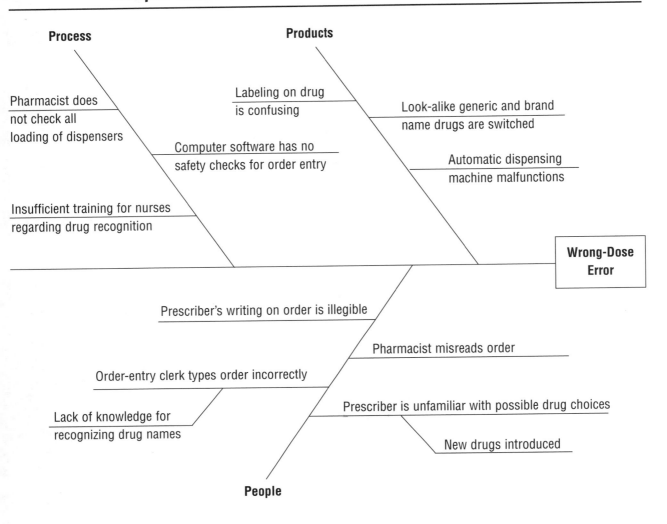

Figure 5-3. *The central axis of this diagram points toward an outcome (wrong-dose errors) with several causes and subcauses that have been separated into groups (branches).*

ing off from the horizontal line. (The cause-and-effect diagram in Figure 5-3, above, uses the general error classification categories—products, process, and people—discussed in Chapter 3.)

3. *List major causes under the general categories.* Brainstorm to identify the major causes. Team members should ask why or how at least five times. Place each main cause on a horizontal line connected to the appropriate diagonal line.

4. *List subcauses and place them under the main causes.* Try to find any relevant causes that contribute to the main causes. Use smaller diagonal lines to connect them to the main causes.

5. *Evaluate the diagram.* The team should study the diagram to determine obvious areas for improvement, causes that are readily solved or eliminated, and areas needing further study so that they can better understand (for example, wrong-dose prescribing errors resulting from a lack of knowledge associated with the introduction of new drugs may be readily solved by providing inservice education about new drugs on a routine basis).

Developing the Implementation Plan

Implementing a successful project depends on a well-designed plan. It is important to collect appropriate data so that you can determine whether a change has been beneficial, and whether future enhancements are feasible. Answering the following questions will help you focus your plan.

1. What is/are the precise aim(s) of your contemplated improvement project (why are you doing this)? Look back at the team's agreed-on goals for the medication use system as a whole for help.

_____

_____

_____

_____

_____

2. How does the contemplated project fit into your organization's framework for performance improvement?

_____

_____

_____

_____

_____

_____

_____

3. Is your proposed project redundant with other projects currently underway in the organization? If yes, what is the extent of the redundancy?

_____

_____

_____

_____

_____

_____

4. What resources will be required to accomplish your proposed project? Be sure to include both financial and human resources.

_____

_____

_____

_____

_____

5. Are these resources available? How will they be obtained?

_____

_____

_____

_____

_____

6. Involvement of your organization's leaders at all stages of the project is critical to the success of the initiative. Identify and list the organization leaders involved in this project and define their roles.

Name/Title   **Role**

_____   _____

_____   _____

_____   _____

_____   _____

_____   _____

_____   _____

_____   _____

7. List the sequential steps necessary to accomplish the proposed improvement project.

a. _____

b. _____

c. _____

d. _____

e. _____

f. _____

g. _____

h. _____

8. Define the time lines and responsibilities associated with each of the project steps using the following table (customize column headers as desired). Questions to consider include: What are the time lines for each step of the project and for the project as a whole? What will be the checkpoints, control points, or milestones for project assessment? Who is responsible for each step or milestone? Who is responsible for corrective course action? What staff members will be involved in the improvement project? What will be the nature and extent of their responsibilities?

Step to Be Taken	Date of Implementation	Areas for Implementation	Individuals Responsible	Other Considerations

9. Who will benefit from this improvement and what will be the nature of the benefit (for example, targeted patient populations, organizational settings, services, departments, staff)? Define the relevance of the improvement for various audiences.

Who Will Benefit

How Will They Benefit

Designing the Measurement Plan

Data are essential to any improvement effort. Without accurate data about how a process is performed, it is not possible to isolate the areas that need improvement. Similarly, if data show problems in the way a process is performed, more data are necessary to help determine or validate the causes underlying that performance. Finally, data are needed to measure the effect of any improvement action. Two key tools are designed to help you collect the data you need: indicators (performance measures), which help define which data to collect, and check sheets and other forms used to collect data related to indicators. The preliminary data collection tools and efforts undertaken to identify the area for improvement may be useful in considering the following questions.

1. What is the scope of measurement for your improvement project? How can you ensure that the project remains focused within its defined scope?

   _____

   _____

   _____

   _____

2. What previous thresholds of the process are being measured? Are there any records of measurements from past studies or portions of the process that are or were measured? If not, can you do a quick, objective (but not necessarily scientific) assessment of the identified cause of the problem? What measurement will you use to determine whether improvement has occurred?

   _____

   _____

   _____

   _____

3. What measurement tools have you decided to use for this initiative? Describe them.

   _____

   _____

_____

_____

_____

4. Is the scope of your identified measurement tool(s) consistent with the defined scope of the project? Why or why not?

_____

_____

_____

_____

_____

5. Are you confident that your selected measurement tool(s) will provide reliable and interpretable data? How do you know?

_____

_____

_____

_____

_____

6. What are the costs associated with collecting the necessary data? Do the benefits of data collection outweigh the costs?

_____

_____

_____

_____

_____

7. Can the data generated by your selected measurement tool be transformed into meaningful and useful information that can be reported in a relevant manner to all stakeholders? What format(s) will you use to report the data?

_____

_____

_____

_____

_____

_____

8. How will you measure the success of this project?

_____

_____

_____

_____

_____

9. Where and how will you obtain any additional data you may need? If you use survey data (for example, for patient satisfaction purposes), the team may have to survey customers. Objective information may be obtained from financial records, administrative data, claims data, medical records, information services, risk management reports, tumor registries, and so forth.

_____

_____

_____

_____

_____

10. What control points or checkpoints exist to ensure that the data are complete and accurate? If the data collection tool has been developed internally, has it been tested? Have indicators been adequately defined, including such things as data elements, allowable values, included/excluded populations, calculation algorithms, sampling procedures, and so on?

_____

_____

_____

_____

_____

11. How do you plan to educate data collection staff? If scientific precision is necessary for the contemplated measurement, you must be sure that qualified personnel are involved in the process.

_____

_____

_____

_____

12. Have you constructed the measurement process to be unbiased? If necessary, have the data been subjected to preliminary validity, reliability, and feasibility studies prior to implementation?

_____

_____

_____

_____

Tools to Use

Indicators. Indicators are quantitative measures of a specific part of a process or of an outcome. More specifically, they are related to one or more dimensions of performance, including efficacy, appropriateness, availability, timeliness, effectiveness, continuity, safety, efficiency, and respect and caring. Indicators by themselves do not directly measure quality. Rather, indicators direct attention to potential performance issues that may require further investigation.

Types of indicators. Indicators can be divided into two general categories: sentinel–event indicators and aggregate–data indicators. A *sentinel-event indicator* records an event that is significant enough to trigger further investigation each time it occurs. For example, any time a patient dies due to a medication error, an investigation will take place.

Aggregate data indicators measure many events. The aggregation of data may be reported in one of two ways—as a continuous variable or as a rate-based (discrete) variable:

- Each value of a *continuous variable indicator* is a precise measurement that can fall anywhere along a continuous scale. An example might be the exact weight in pounds of an individual receiving total parenteral nutrition.

- The value of a measurement of a *rate-based indicator* reflects the frequency of an event or condition and is expressed as a proportion or a ratio. A *proportion* shows the number of occurrences over the entire group within which the occurrence could take place (for example, errors reported for patients self-administering medication over all medications administered). A *ratio* shows occurrences compared with a different but related phenomenon (for example, wrong-dose errors for diabetic patients over patients receiving insulin).

Using indicators. Indicators should be phrased as complete and objective statements that can be answered with a specific measurement or indication of whether the event in question occurred. The validity and reliability of all data and subsequent data displays depend on the clarity and specificity of your indicators. There must be no room for individual interpretation during data collection. Teams may want to consult an expert in statistics and/or performance measurement to make sure their selected indicators are feasible. Table 1-2 from Chapter 1 (pages 14–15) lists the medication use indicators approved for use in the IMSystem performance measurement system.

Check sheets. Check sheets are simple tools that show how many times a given event occurs. They are the most basic statistical tool, used to record data that answer objective statements requiring a simple yes or no response. Follow these steps to create a check sheet:

1. *Agree on the data to be collected.* To reach a consensus, the team needs to have already studied the process; it may also need to brainstorm and multivote. Remember to phrase the clearest possible statements about which data to collect. When considering what data will be collected, the team must consider the data source. Will the information be in patient records? Will it be observed firsthand?

2. *Decide on the time period for collection.* The team must decide how long a period will be necessary for the information to be reliable—one day, one week, one month, and so on. Also, the team needs to choose

Sample Check Sheet: Transcription Errors

	Week 1	Week 2	Week 3	Week 4	Week 5	Week 6	Week 7
1st Floor	‖	‖|			‖	—	‖		
2nd Floor	‖|	‖	‖|			‖	‖|	‖
3rd Floor	✔✔✔✔	‖|	‖|	‖|	‖‖	‖	‖|
Dementia Unit	—			‖|	‖	‖			—
Hospice Unit	‖	‖|	—	‖|	‖				

Figure 5-4. *This check sheet format allows staff members to record how many transcription errors occurred in each area of a long term care organization over a seven-week period. This helps to pinpoint areas where improvement is needed.*

the time of day for collections; for example, all shifts, days only, evenings only. The team should consider the effects of collecting data during particular months or on particular days of the week.

3. *Select a sample size, if appropriate.* Often, the sample size for a check sheet study is 100%; in other words, all relevant situations or medications are included. Some high-volume events may make recording every relevant situation impractical. If this is the case, the team may need to select a random, representative sample of at least 20%. It is crucial that the sample be statistically reliable.

4. *Decide who will collect the data.* Data collectors must be knowledgeable enough about the process in question to reliably collect the information. They may do it as part of their everyday tasks (concurrent), or separately using other documents (retrospective). Ideally, those who actually collect the data will help design the check sheet.

5. *Design the check sheet.* The form should be clear and easy to use. It should include a place for the date, time, name of the data collector, and comments, and give plenty of space for entering the data. Figure 5-4 (above) shows a sample check sheet.

6. *Test the check sheet.* One way to test a check sheet is to have one or two people who did not help design the form use it. Use their feedback to make any necessary changes to the form.

7. *Distribute the check sheet and collect the data.* Distribute copies to all data collectors; they will then collect data until the end of the specified period. Make certain that collection is done consistently and accurately.

8. *Tally all individual data sheets.* Use a single sheet to tally all information from the individual check sheets. The totals may be aggregated by day, shift, week, month, occurrence, and so on.

9. *Evaluate the data.* The results of data collection may indicate areas that require further attention. For example, from a list of potential problems, one may occur frequently and the others rarely. The tools described in the data analysis section of this chapter can help you take the data beyond their raw form so the team can draw conclusions and take action.

Data Analysis

The team already used informal data analysis methods to determine which project should be undertaken. However, once the team has collected data about the identified process, more structured tools for data analysis will be useful.

Often, data analysis involves some form of comparison between current findings and previous (baseline) findings, or current findings may be compared to established standards, critical path specifications, or "best practices" (benchmarking). The run chart is familiar to health care professionals and one of the simplest tools to construct and use. It can be used during problem identification, data analysis, and result evaluation, or any time a team needs a simple visual display of performance trends over a specific period of time. Many other data analysis tools may also be useful to you at this stage, including control charts, histograms, and scatter diagrams (see the "Tools to Use" section on pages 101–108). These tools should satisfy most of your in-house data analysis needs, but if you need more ideas or information, the bibliography at the end of this chapter will help you identify relevant resources. Consider the data that will be generated from your performance improvement project as you review these tools and select the one(s) that is most appropriate for tracking and presenting your data.

1. Which data analysis tools will you use for your improvement initiative?

   a. _____

   b. _____

   c. _____

   d. _____

2. Describe which data will be collected over what period of time.

   _____

   _____

   _____

   _____

3. What format(s) will you use to report data/findings? Is there an "organizational format" for reporting performance improvement data? Does your organization have standards for the use of tabular, narrative, or graphic output to communicate performance improvement information? How can the output be presented to ensure clarity for all users?

_____

_____

_____

_____

4. Does your organization have a communication plan? How are other performance improvement initiatives communicated? How often do you expect to communicate? Is there a central storyboard? Is it communicated in newsletters, departmental meetings, crossdepartmental meetings, inter- and intradepartmental memoranda? Are the data readily accessible and retrievable for all bonafide users?

_____

_____

_____

_____

5. To whom will data/findings be reported?

Name	Title
_____	_____
_____	_____
_____	_____
_____	_____
_____	_____

Tools to Use

Control Charts. Control charts are run charts that include statistically determined limits on either side of the average or mean. Control charts are designed to show what type of variation exists in a process and whether the process is statistically "in control." A variables control chart measures quantitative data such as time or length, whereas an attributes control chart measures qualitative data such as an error rate.

Control charts are used to identify problems, analyze data, and evaluate results of an improvement action; they are useful whenever a team needs to know whether the variation in a process is common (inherent in the way the process is designed and performed) or is caused by unique events or individual actions. Generally, control charts are used to track performance over a significant period of time; thus, they may not be appropriate for short-term improvement projects.

Control charts involve complex statistical rules, and it is necessary to consult a textbook, handbook, or other source of statistics expertise to fully understand how to create them. Please see the appendix to *Using Performance Improvement Tools in Health Care Settings,* published by the Joint Commission, for a more detailed explanation than the basic steps of control chart construction shown here.

1. *Choose a process to evaluate and obtain a data set.* For the purposes of this explanation, we will assume that the team already has studied the process and has obtained a data set of at least 15 to 20 data points using a check sheet or another collection tool. For the steps that follow, it is important that the data were obtained before any adjustments were made to the process.

2. *Calculate the mean.* The mean (also called the average) of a data set provides a reference point that shows the central tendency of a data distribution. To obtain the mean, divide the sum of all measurements by the total number of measurements in the data set.

3. *Calculate the standard deviation and set upper and lower control limits.* The *standard deviation* of a data set is the measure of its variability. Consult a source of statistics expertise to aid in calculating the standard deviation. Typically, the control limits are one to three times higher or lower than the standard deviation relative to the mean. For example, say the mean is 31 and the standard deviation is 5. If you set control limits at twice the standard deviation (plus or minus 10), the upper control limit would be 41 and the lower limit would be 21.

4. *Create the control chart.* Plot the horizontal and vertical axes the way you would for a run chart. On the chart, plot the mean and the upper and lower control limits. Refer to Figure 5-5 (page 102) to see how the chart should look.

5. *Plot the data.* As is done for a run chart, the next step is to plot the correct measurements for each point in time, remembering to keep the data in the same sequence in which they were collected. Connect the points with a line to show the performance trends and patterns.

6. *Analyze the chart and investigate findings.* First, determine whether the process is statistically in or out of control. A process must be in control before overall performance can be improved. If the data points fall within the control limits, then the causes of variation are considered common (or random) and the process is in control. If points fall above or below the limits, the process is out of control. This

Sample Control Charts

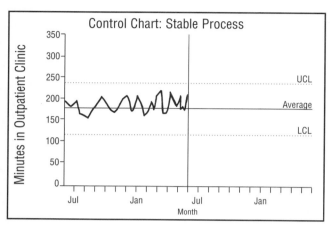

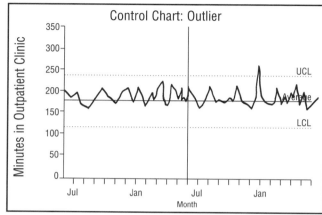

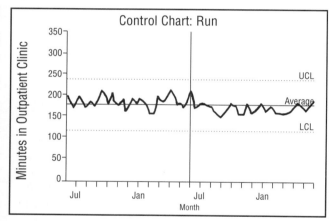

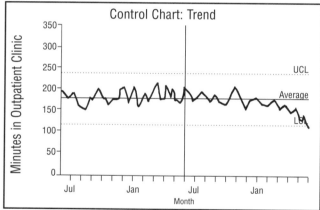

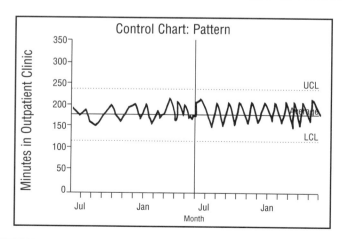

Figure 5–5. *This series of control charts illustrates different patterns of performance an organization is likely to encounter.*

means that the variation is caused by special, unpredictable events and the process needs more immediate investigation.

When a process is out of control, try to determine why.[1] Has there been a significant change in the environment? Were any untrained workers involved in the process at the time? Has there been a change in equipment maintenance? Special causes must be eliminated before the process can be fundamentally improved and before the control chart can be used as a monitoring tool.

7. *Remember that the terms "in control" and "out of control" do not signify whether a process meets the desired level of performance.* These are statistical definitions that refer to whether a process is consistent. A process may be in control, but may be consistently poor in terms of quality, and the converse may be true.

Figure 5–5 shows five examples of patterns or trends that might be shown by a control chart. The scenarios are as follows:

- *Stable process.* All points are within the control limits. The process is thus stable or in control.

- *Outlier.* One point jumps outside the control limit. Staff should determine whether this single occurrence is likely to recur.

- *Run.* A run occurs when a given number of points in a row are on one or the other side of the average. This may suggest an opportunity for improvement.

- *Trend.* A trend is a steady rise or fall in performance. Trends headed toward or crossing control limits suggest that further assessment is necessary.

- *Pattern.* An identifiable pattern in performance, such as the one shown here, may indicate a performance problem associated with factors such as shift, patient population, and so forth.

Histograms. Histograms are essentially bar charts that display patterns of variation in a set of data. They display the way measurement data are distributed. Histograms are valuable tools for the data analysis and result evaluation stages of performance improvement. They address issues such as how much and what kind of variation exists in a process. By studying the results, your team can determine whether the variation is normal and identify target areas that need further attention.

This process may seem a bit more complex than others. Follow these steps carefully to minimize confusion and build an accurate histogram. For more detailed information, you may need to consult a statistics textbook or an expert in statistics.

1. *Obtain the data set and count the number of data points.* Collect all the data you wish to analyze and count each item as a data point. For example, in Figure 5–6 (page 104) a team constructed a histogram to represent the average time it took for a hospital pharmacy to fill orders for a long term care unit once the orders were received. The team counted 50 data points.

2. *Determine the range for the entire data set.* Find the largest (90) and smallest (41) values in your data set. Subtract the smallest value from the largest value. This will give the range ($R = 51$).

Sample Histogram: Turnaround Time for Dispensing of Medication

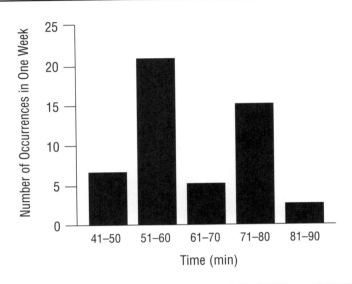

Figure 5-6. *This histogram is used to analyze the variation in average time elapsed for dispensing medications to a long term care unit once the pharmacy receives orders. The irregular distribution suggests opportunities for improvement.*

3. *Set the number of classes into which the data will be divided.* The classes will make the bars of the histogram. Use the following guide to determine the number of classes (represented by the letter K):[2]

Number of Data Points	Number of Classes (K)
≤ 50	5–7
51–100	6–10
100–250	7–12
More than 250	10–20

The example in Figure 5-6 has 50 data points and 5 classes.

4. *Determine the class width.* To determine how wide each bar will be, divide the range (R) by the number of classes (K). The resulting number, rounded off, will be the width (W) of each class or bar in the histogram. Using this formula, the example's class width is set at 10.

5. *Establish class boundaries.* Class boundaries are the starting and ending points of the bars on the histogram. To establish the boundaries, use the following procedure:

- Take the smallest number in the data set and round it down, if necessary. This number (41 in the example) marks the lower boundary of the first class.

- Add the class width (10) to the lower boundary value of the first class. This gives you the lower boundary of the second class (41 + 10 = 51). Data set values from 41 to 50 are included in the first class.

- Continue adding the value for W to each lower value to determine the parameters for all the classes.

- Be sure that the classes are mutually exclusive, so that each data point will fit into one and only one class.

In the example, the classes are as follows:

Class	Range
1	41–50
2	51–60
3	61–70
4	71–80
5	81–90

6. *Construct the histogram.* Place the values for the classes on the horizontal axis and the frequency along the vertical axis.

7. *Count the data points in each class and create the bars.* Count how many occurrences (the number of data points) fall into each class, then draw bars of the appropriate height to indicate the frequency of each class on the graph. Refer to Figure 5-6.

8. *Analyze the findings.* In most cases, small variation is ideal, provided it is within your specifications. Note the amount of variability, then check to see whether the curve made by the tops of the bars is centered or if it is skewed left or right. Large variation or skewed distribution may signal that the process requires further attention. Keep in mind, however, that some processes are naturally skewed, and don't expect a "normal" pattern every time.

   Also look for double peaks, as seen in Figure 5-6 at the second and fourth classes. They suggest that the variation should be reduced and that further information should be gathered about the turn-around times in the 71- to 80-minute range; the fluctuations may be accounted for by shift changes or other considerations.

Scatter Diagrams. Scatter diagrams are graphs designed to show the statistical correlation (but not necessarily the cause-and-effect relationship) between two variables. Use the following process to create a scatter diagram:

1. *Decide which two variables will be tested.* The team should select two variables it suspects are related. For example, in Figure 5-7, page 106, the number of medications taken by each patient and the patient's age are examined for reported errors pertaining to self-administration.

2. *Collect and record relevant data.* Gather 50 to 100 paired samples of data involving each of the variables and record them on a data sheet. (This is not the actual construction of the diagram.)

Sample Scatter Diagram: Variables Correlating in Self-Administration Errors

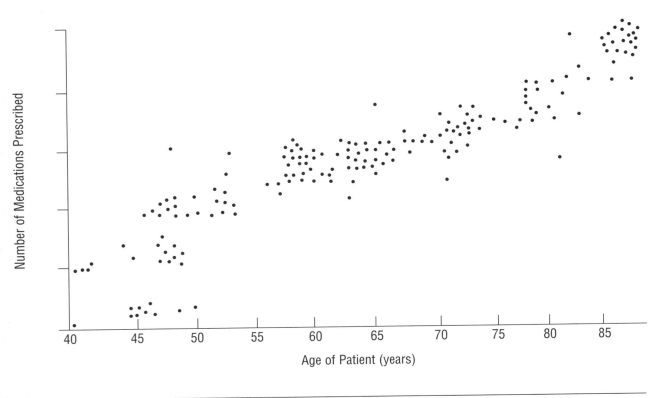

Figure 5-7. *This scatter diagram compares two variables associated with self-administration errors—the number of medications prescribed and the ages of the patients involved. As might be expected, the clustering of points shows that the older the patient, the higher the number of medications involved in care.*

3. *Draw the horizontal and vertical axes.* Usually, the horizontal (*x*) axis represents the variable you suspect is the cause, and the vertical (*y*) axis represents the effect. In our example, the *x* axis represents the patients' ages, and the *y* axis represents the number of medications prescribed for each patient.

4. *Plot the variables on the graph.* Referring back to your data-collection sheet, mark the appropriate intersecting points on the graph. If a value is repeated, circle that point as many times as necessary.

5. *Interpret the completed diagram.* Certain conclusions may be drawn according to the way the points cluster on the graph.[1] Remember, if the diagram indicates a relationship, it is not necessarily a cause-and-effect relationship:

- The more the clusters form a straight line, the stronger the relationship between the two variables.

- If points cluster in an area running from lower left to upper right, the two variables have a positive correlation.

Sample Run Chart: Order-Entry Errors

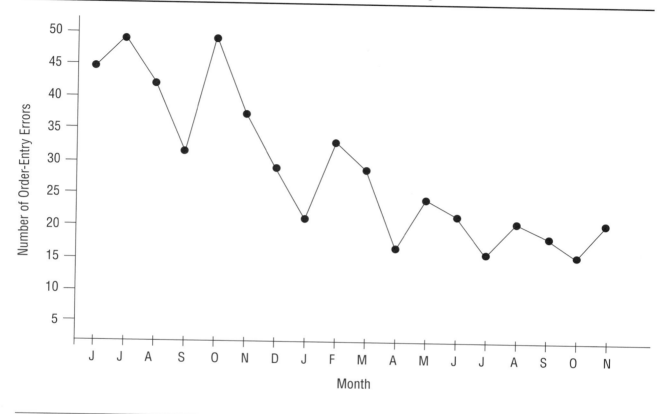

Figure 5-8. *Run charts display levels of performance over time—in this case, the average number of computer order-entry errors made by home health agency staff over an 18-month period. Early numbers are understandably erratic due to the initiation of a new computer system.*

- If points cluster from upper left to lower right, the variables have a negative correlation.
- If points are scattered all over the diagram, these variables may not have any correlation.

Run Charts. A run chart plots points on a graph to show levels of performance over time. This allows the team to spot trends, cycles, and patterns, which is crucial to identifying which areas need improvement and when conditions are improving. Follow these steps to create a run chart:

1. *Decide what the chart will measure.* Determine what data will be collected and over what period of time (for example, the pharmacy will track the number of order-entry errors over a period of 18 months). The time period used should be long enough to show a trend.

2. *Draw the graph's axes.* The horizontal (*x*) axis should indicate time or sequence, and the vertical (*y*) axis should indicate what is being studied in increments, as shown in Figure 5-8, above. Be sure to mark all units of measurement clearly on the chart.

3. *Plot the data points for each point in time and connect them with a line.* You may want to indicate on the chart any significant changes or events that occur during the time period you are studying. This can be done by drawing and labeling dashed lines through the chart at the appropriate points on the x axis.

4. *Evaluate the chart to identify meaningful trends.* You may want to seek expert statistical advice for this task. Above all, keep in mind that the purpose of this tool is to help you focus on trends and patterns in the process; do not be overly concerned with any one particular point on the chart. The following are some key concepts to consider when analyzing the chart:

   - An equal number of points will fall above and below the average; this is how the average is calculated.

   - A "run" of six or more points on one side of the average indicates a statistically unusual event or a shift.

   - A trend of six or more steadily increasing or decreasing points (with no reversals) also indicates an important change.

   - Annual cycles, such as when most staff take vacations during the year, should be considered.

5. *Investigate the findings.* Any time your findings indicate a notable trend or pattern, the team should investigate further to determine the cause of the movement. If the change or shift represented in the chart is favorable, it should become part of the system. If the shift is unfavorable, the team should take additional action to improve performance.

Implementing and Monitoring Performance Improvement

Once you have your project plan established, the time has come to implement it. You begin with a pilot test, determine whether your system has improved, and then monitor the improvement to maintain it and learn from your success.

Pilot Testing the Improvement

It is wisest to implement your project on a small scale at first and thoroughly study the results prior to full-scale implementation. This approach allows for validation or refinement of the improvement actions before they are applied to your entire organization. This is of particular importance when your proposed actions require a large investment of organizational resources. Consider the following questions relative to the small-scale or pilot test.

1. Which area(s) will be used for the pilot test? Why are these areas preferable over other possible areas?

_____

_____

_____

_____

_____

2. Do pilot test data indicate that the actions had a positive impact? If so, describe the extent of the change. If not, do the data identify other ways to impact/improve the process? What are they?

_____

_____

_____

_____

_____

_____

3. How does postpilot data compare with prepilot data?

_____

_____

_____

_____

_____

_____

4. What other benchmarking databases exist for comparison purposes relative to this project? Are there internal as well as external databases? Do any professional organizations have this type of comparative data?

a. _____

b. _____

c. _____

d. _____

e. _____

5. Is the team completely satisfied with the improvement? Has the maximum level of achievement in the identified area been realized? If not, how can the approach be improved before full-scale implementation?

_____

_____

_____

_____

_____

6. Are there improvements to be made, based on the pilot test, to increase the efficiency of monitoring (that is, data collection and data analysis)? Can you decrease monitoring frequency while maintaining the quality of the analysis required to maintain the integrity of the project?

_____

_____

_____

_____

_____

Monitoring the Improvement

Once small-scale or pilot testing has been completed and the team is satisfied that the improvement/ intervention is having the desired impact, the implementation of the improvement can be expanded to include all relevant areas. Continued monitoring of the process, however, is essential to ensure that the improvement can be sustained over time and will support the identification of other areas for improvement. More intensive measurement in the early stages of improvement implementation is needed to ensure that full-scale implementation is yielding the same results as experienced in the pilot testing phase. However, once the desired state (for example, rate) is achieved, measurement activities can be less intensive. Consider the following questions relative to your ongoing monitoring activities.

1. According to your performance goals, what percentage of "change" (for example, number of defects, rates) is an acceptable measure of process improvement (now and in the future)?

_____

_____

_____

_____

_____

2. Is the change in process as measured in outcome benefit what you expected? If not, why not? What can be done to address the shortfall?

_____

_____

_____

_____

_____

3. If the data are represented on a control chart, is there a relationship between the time the change was implemented and the change in measurement rates? Explain.

_____

_____

_____

_____

_____

4. What monitoring mechanisms do you have to ensure that the process is not left to run itself? Is the frequency of monitoring compatible with the frequency of occurrence for the process being measured? Does this require continuous or discontinuous monitoring? Is it automated, or does a person have to go to the process change point every time an event occurs and gather the data to be collected?

_____

_____

_____

_____

_____

_____

_____

5. If multiple locations are affected by the improvement, are there differences in results among locations? If so, why do you think this has occurred? How will you address this issue?

_____

_____

_____

_____

_____

_____

_____

Modifying Your Current Medication Use System to Reflect Improvement(s)

The final step in the improvement process is to codify the improvement you have achieved to ensure that it is sustained in the organization. Codification of the improvement may have multiple components, depending on its nature. Consider the following when determining what actions are needed to permanently incorporate the improvement into your organization.

1. Modify the original flowchart of your organization's medication use system to incorporate the improvement actions.

2. Do the changes as represented in the updated/revised flowchart require modification of existing organizational procedures or protocols or the development of new procedures or protocols? If so, what are they? Who will be responsible for handling this task? What approvals are necessary?

_____

_____

_____

_____

_____

3. Do the changes represented in the updated/revised flowchart require modification of existing organizational policies or the development of new policies? If so, what are they? Who will be responsible for handling this task? What approvals are necessary?

_____

_____

_____

_____

_____

4. How will full-scale implementation of this initiative be communicated throughout your organization? Who needs to know? What communication vehicles will you use? Will communication be varied depending on the audience (that is, those directly versus those indirectly affected by the improvement)?

_____

_____

_____

_____

5. Is there a need for training relative to the improvement (for example, relative to new procedures)? If so, who should receive the training? Who should conduct the training? How will this training be incorporated into routine on-the-job-training for new hires?

_____

_____

_____

_____

_____

6. What kind of training materials will need to be developed? Who will be responsible for this task?

_____

_____

_____

_____

_____

7. Does this improvement initiative qualify for the Joint Commission's Ernest A. Codman Award (see sidebar, page 115)? If so, who will be responsible for completing the application? What approvals are needed?

_____

_____

_____

_____

_____

The Ernest A. Codman Award

The Ernest A. Codman Award, sponsored by the Joint Commission in cooperation with Pfizer Inc, is presented to health care organizations for achievements in the use of process and outcomes measures to improve organization performance and, ultimately, the quality of care provided to the public. Named for the physician regarded in health care as the "father of outcomes measurement," the Ernest A. Codman Award has been created to showcase the effective use of performance measures, thereby enhancing knowledge and encouraging the use of performance measurement to improve the quality of health care. For more information about the award program or application and evaluation process, please contact the Joint Commission's Customer Service Center at (630)792-5800.

Assessment of Other Areas for Improvement

Successful implementation of one project should lead to the identification of other areas for improvement within the process you are currently addressing. In addition, the preliminary work you did to identify the current area for improvement also targeted other critical areas of the system that needed improvement. Review the findings from this improvement project and the work you did in the preparation and planning sections of this chapter to determine where your next focus should be. If you wish to look at another system, use the information you already have, but be sure to begin by developing a flowchart of the new system and then selectively moving through the subsequent steps.

The guidelines in this chapter will help you begin activities to improve your medication use system. The questions and exercises are simply a starting point. As you select the process or stage in the system you wish to address, you will come up with more specific questions and find yourself building on the basics provided here. Familiarize yourself with at least some of the resources listed at the end of the chapter and you will find even more ideas. Like any other system, performance improvement can always be refined.

Now that you have read about systems, measuring and monitoring medication use, defining and preventing medication errors, and improving your medication use system, you will be able to see all of this information applied to an actual health care organization in Chapter 6.

Reference

1. GOAL/QPC: *The Memory Jogger.* Methuen, MA: GOAL/QPC, 1988, p 46.

First Do No Harm

A PRACTICAL GUIDE TO MEDICATION SAFETY AND JCAHO COMPLIANCE

Table of Contents

ORDER YOUR COPY TODAY!

First Do No Harm: A Practical Guide to Medication Safety and JCAHO Compliance

ORDER CARD

If you subscribe to any Opus Communications publication, you will receive a special discount!

TITLE	PRICE	DISCOUNT PRICE	QUANTITY	TOTAL
First Do No Harm	❏ $87 (MEDN)	❏ $79 (MED)		
*Your order is fully covered by a 30-day, money-back guarantee. *Shipping to AK, HI, Puerto Rico, and Canada is $19.95.*			Shipping*	$9.00
			Grand Total	

SHIP TO: (Shipments CANNOT be delivered to P.O. boxes.)

Name _____

Title _____

Organization _____

Street Address _____

City _____ State _____ ZIP _____

Telephone (_____) _____ Fax (_____) _____

E-mail Address_____

Anticipated date of next JCAHO survey: Month _____ Year _____

If other than JCAHO, please specify: _____

Source code: B4396 W A B C D E F G

BILLING OPTIONS:

❏ Check enclosed (payable to Opus Communications).

❏ Bill my organization with PO # _____.

❏ Bill me.

❏ Bill my: VISA/MasterCard/AmEx (circle one).

Signature _____
(Required for authorization)

Account # _____

Exp. Date _____
(Your credit card bill will reflect a charge to Opus Communications.)

Opus Communications	200 Hoods Lane, P.O. Box 1168, Marblehead, MA 01945		
Telephone: 800/650-6787	Fax: 800/639-8511	E-mail: customer_service@opuscomm.com	Internet: www.opuscomm.com

8/99

Copyright 1999 Opus Communications.
Opus Communications is not affiliated in any way with the Joint Commission on Accreditation of Healthcare Organizations.

Chapter 6

CASE STUDY ON MEASURING AND IMPROVING THE MEDICATION USE SYSTEM

P Mardi Atkins, RN, MPA
Manager, Nursing Quality Management
The Cleveland Clinic Foundation
Cleveland, Ohio

Louis D Barone
Department of Pharmacy
The Cleveland Clinic Foundation
Cleveland, Ohio

Medication administration is the most frequently repeated action in an acute care setting. Most patients entering a hospital receive a dose of medication at least one time while there. The routes of administration have expanded beyond the traditional oral, intramuscular, subcutaneous, and intravenous (IV) routes to include medications given by epidural, intracranial, and transdermal routes. Administration procedures have become more complex, and the need for more intense monitoring of the effects of drugs is growing proportionately.

Medication use systems consist of policies and procedures, drug formularies and references, and checks and balances. All aspects of these systems require ongoing monitoring to ensure the accuracy of medication administration. The health care organization with a comprehensive monitoring system can identify where the potential for errors or inefficiencies exists and the type of actions needed to decrease the risk. This chapter presents an overview of one group practice's medication use system and efforts made at the various process stages to improve the system.

Background

The Cleveland Clinic Foundation (CCF) is a large tertiary care group practice with a 1,000-bed acute care hospital. Approximately 700 staff physicians provide services in 38 specialties from primary care to complex medical and surgical diagnoses. The hospital admits over 40,000 patients per year and has 1 million annual ambulatory clinic visits. Eleven thousand employees work in the hospital, ambulatory clinics, research, and the satellite family health centers.

The hospital nursing department comprises over 2,000 licensed and unlicensed caregivers and clerical staff. Inpatient services are provided on specialty-based medical surgical units, intensive care units (ICUs), and psychiatric units, as well as in pediatrics and obstetrical services. The overall responsibility for the quality of care lies with the chairman of the division of nursing.

The pharmacy department provides comprehensive pharmaceutical services for patients in the hospital 24 hours a day, 7 days a week. The inpatient pharmacy department includes pharmacists dedicated to clinical/patient care roles, with administrative, technical, and clerical support personnel. The nucleus of the clinical pharmacy services are the pharmaceutical care specialists, typically trained pharmacists at the doctoral level (PharmD), who help to formulate and develop clinical initiatives and practice guidelines for the pharmacy staff.

The medical executive committee, composed of the chairs from the organization's various divisions—such as medicine, surgery, and nursing—serves as the quality steering board, setting the organizationwide priorities for improvement and determining the resource allocation to meet these goals. The Office of Quality Management (OQM) has oversight of the organization's quality management program and regulatory agency standards compliance. The general counsel's office, the OQM, nursing quality manager, and ambulatory nursing manager meet regularly to discuss risk management issues and concerns and to identify actions or plans to reduce the organization's risk. This group also oversees the sentinel event process.

When quality improvement began migrating into the health care arena, CCF decided to diversify its approach. To implement quality improvement, it taught managers to use quality improvement tools such as flowcharts, cause-and-effect diagrams, force field analyses, and various types of control charts in their daily management activities. Just-in-time training is done when a team is formed to design or revise a process. Each department has an internal quality structure responsible for coordinating projects and reporting activities to the OQM.

CCF also implemented a nursing–pharmacy liaison group to serve as a forum for communication and decision making regarding the medication distribution and administration processes. The group consists of pharmacy and nursing personnel at both managerial and staff levels. Typically, subgroups are formed to address specific goals, projects, and policy development. The aim of this group is to eliminate the duplication and contradictions that can exist between policies developed for nursing, pharmacy, and other areas within the organization. For example, 25 different policies from other departments were found to vary from the official pharmacy and nursing policies. The intensive care units, anesthesia, and some specialty groups such as cardiology had developed their own policies, because the pharmacy and nursing policies did not meet the needs of their patient populations. When the policies were compared, only slight variations existed; some simply addressed exceptions to the official policies. A single policy was developed by the nursing–pharmacy liaison group and approved by the pharmacy and therapeutics (P&T) committee and the other medical groups involved.

The liaison group has been charged with developing organizationwide medication use policies to be added to the policy and procedure manual on CCF's intranet. The group ensures that the policies limit the potential for adverse drug events (ADEs). With 4.5 million doses of medications dispensed throughout the organization each year, the medication use system must be efficient and have checks and balances in place to ensure accuracy and to quickly identify problem areas.

The Medication Use System

The multidisciplinary P&T committee oversees the medication use system. This is a standing committee defined in the organization's bylaws and reports to the medical executive committee. Its members are appointed by the chairman of the P&T committee and approved by the medical executive committee and the board of governors. The P&T committee serves as the formal line of communication among the medical staff, the pharmacy, and the nursing department. Its other organizationwide functions include the following:

- Approving policies and procedures that govern the evaluation, selection, procurement, control, distribution, and administration of drugs in the hospital;

- Maintaining a current formulary and drug therapy guide by evaluating and selecting drugs based on critical and objective evaluation of their therapeutic merits, safety, and cost, with emphasis on minimizing generic and therapeutic duplication;

- Performing drug use evaluation to assess the safe, effective, and appropriate use of drugs in the hospital;

- Reviewing problems involving the safe distribution and administration of drugs, including reported adverse drug reactions (ADRs) and medication errors;

- Providing all health professionals with current information on drugs and their use through publications, computer systems, and educational programs;

- Supporting the development of contemporary, innovative pharmaceutical services and systems in the hospital;

- Promoting cost-effective drug therapy without compromising the quality of medical care; and

- Maintaining an awareness of the activities of pharmaceutical company representatives within the facility and recommending corrective actions as necessary.

Ordering Process

In large organizations, automating patient care processes can be slow due to the complex factors that need to be considered, such as interfacing with existing systems, the amount of hardware required, and wiring within existing buildings. This is the case with CCF's medication use system. After many years in development, the organization began automating its ordering and transcribing processes in 1998. Automated medication distribution technologies are being identified and selected to support these processes.

In the interim, much effort has been made to ensure that manual processes are as effective and efficient as possible. Medications are dispensed and administered to patients only on the written order of a physician with appropriate medical staff privileges. All orders for medications must be documented on the physician order form in the patient's medical record and dated, time stamped, and signed by the prescriber. Telephone and verbal orders are strongly discouraged, except in cases of emergency or when in the best interests of the patient.

Transcription

Transcribing medication orders is the responsibility of a unit secretary and a registered nurse. The manual process is proposed to be automated in 1998. After the physician writes the order, the unit secretary transcribes it onto the medication administration record. The secretary then flags the chart to indicate the order has been transcribed, removes the carbon copy of the order, and places it in the pharmacy pick-up basket. Orders may be faxed to the pharmacy to expedite processing. If the order is stat, the secretary is responsible for notifying the registered nurse. The nurse is responsible for verifying the accuracy of the transcribed order. New orders are not initiated until this verification step is completed.

Physicians are encouraged to avoid using abbreviations that can be misinterpreted. For example, with insulin orders, *unit* must be spelled out instead of being abbreviated as "u." This recommendation was made after several insulin events were reported after the "u" was misinterpreted as a zero and "4 units" was read as "40 units."

Preparing and Dispensing

A unit-dose medication distribution system is used on all inpatient units, and medication carts are refilled every 24 hours. When a medication order is received in the pharmacy, a pharmacist reviews it for appropriateness prior to dispensing (the only exception is an emergency situation when time is limited). The pharmacy dispenses an initial supply of medication intended to last until the next "fill." The registered nurse ensures that the medications issued by the pharmacy are consistent with those transcribed. Any discrepancy at this point may be an indication of a differing interpretation of the order or a transcription or dispensing error. The nurse takes steps to resolve such discrepancies with the pharmacist.

After this initial fill, a new 24-hour supply of medication is dispensed each morning. Any unused medications are returned to the pharmacy and credited to the patient's account. Most important, returns of discontinued medication eliminate the potential for the patient to receive the wrong dose or the wrong drug. Unit-of-use packaging is used wherever possible for oral, injectable, and topical products. The intravenous admixture service prepares antibiotics, electrolytes, pain management, cancer chemotherapy products, total parenteral nutrition, and other specialty formulations for all inpatients.

Compliance with procedures of the unit-dose distribution system is essential to ensure that checks and balances are maintained. For example, borrowing of medications and excessive use of floor stock medications are discouraged because both eliminate the pharmacist as a check point. An effective and efficient medication distribution system must be in place to minimize these temptations.

Pharmacists review approximately 1 million medication orders at CCF annually, resulting in 3.8 million unit doses and 730,000 IV admixtures administered. All medications are checked for accuracy by a pharmacist against the original order prior to initial dispensing. Any questions identified during the course of this process—such as those relating to therapeutic appropriateness, dosing, allergies, drug interactions, or disease state interactions—are resolved before the medication is dispensed. The pharmacist makes the appropriate changes to the medication order, and the unit is notified of the order change when the medication is dispensed. The registered nurse makes the change on the medication administration record and places the notification slip in the patient's chart before the drug is administered. Pharmacy staff logs information on the number of physician clarifications requested, and a review of this log indicates how many potential medication errors were avoided because of this step.

Administration

Nurses have drug reference books and an online drug information system, as well as a pharmacist available to answer any questions that may arise with medication administration. Registered nurses and licensed practical nurses (LPNs) can administer medications. The LPN is limited to administration of topical, oral, and injectable (not intravenous) medications. Administration of the medication is considered timely if it is administered between 30 minutes before and 30 minutes after the scheduled time. A registered nurse is responsible for medication administration to six to eight patients on a medical–surgical unit and one to three patients on the intensive care unit.

Each medical–surgical unit has two to three medication carts, each with 12 to 14 patient drawers, located in close proximity to the patients' rooms. This plan has successfully eliminated the congestion at the medication cart during heavy-traffic administration times. It has also decreased the practice of pre-preparing medications and "storing" them elsewhere, such as in the clean utility room, to avoid the congestion at the medication cart. Consequently, the number of ADEs related to wrong time and omission because the nurse "wasn't able to get to the medication cart and then got busy" has decreased.

Nursing staff do not confirm medication dosages with another nurse, except in cases of experimental drugs and certain medications in the pediatric and obstetric areas. Although insulin and heparin traditionally had to be confirmed before administration, discontinuing this practice did not increase the number of ADEs involved with these medications.

Monitoring

Physicians have primary responsibility for monitoring the effects of medications, but are very dependent on the observations of registered nurses. In the past two to three years, more responsibility has been delegated to the nursing staff for monitoring and regulating medication doses. For example, the changes in the doses for patient-controlled analgesia are based on nursing observations of the patient's pain level and the number of attempts for medication in a given time frame. In certain areas, heparin doses are regulated based on bedside clotting test results. Sliding-scale insulin doses are based on the results of bedside blood glucose meter results. Drug levels are scheduled by the nursing staff, and in some areas, the blood sample is drawn by the nursing staff to ensure the correct time span. Nurses are the primary data collectors and their accuracy is key in helping patients achieve therapeutic dose levels.

Clinical pharmacists also have recently expanded their role in medication monitoring by participating directly in patient care rounds with physicians. They can make suggestions for appropriate medication and dosing. The benefit of this practice has been a decrease in the number of order clarifications needed and a proactive opportunity for implementation of P&T committee drug utilization activities.

Certain medications require that drug levels or laboratory values be determined in defined time frames and that adjustments of the drug dosage be made accordingly. An example might be primary organ function monitoring to ensure appropriate dosing of drugs such as aminoglycosides and theophylline. The clinical pharmacist's knowledge of drug distribution and metabolism often allows for more appropriate initial dosing, resulting in more timely therapeutic drug levels and/or minimization of potential toxicities.

Incident Reporting System

One of the adverse drug events tracked by the incident reporting system is "medication events" (CCF's term for medication errors). A *medication event* is defined as any event in which the patient did not receive the medication as ordered. The organization uses the definitions approved by the American Society of Health-System Pharmacists (ASHP; see Chapter 3) to define the types of medication events. The most frequently reported types of events are omission, unauthorized drug, and wrong rate. Incident reports are written by the person responsible for the error or the person who discovers it. The process for reporting an event is illustrated in Figure 6-1, page 122.

Quality improvement methodologies stress looking at systems and processes rather than individuals; improvement efforts can be successful only if employees are not afraid to report errors. Organizations must drive out the fear of retalia-

Process for Reporting an Adverse Drug Event

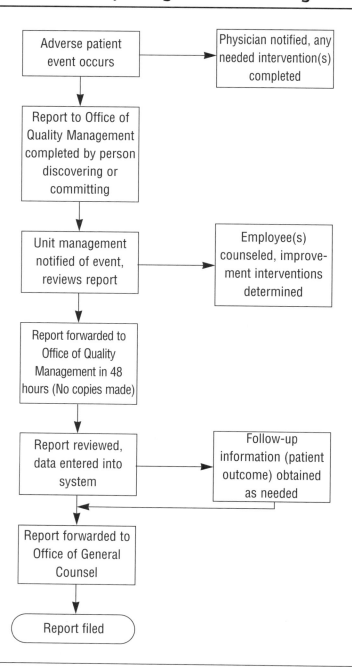

Figure 6-1. *This flowchart illustrates the procedure used at The Cleveland Clinic Foundation to report adverse drug reactions, or "medication events." Reporting is encouraged by assuring staff that reports are used for quality improvement purposes, rather than to lay blame on individuals.*

Source: The Cleveland Clinic Foundation, Ohio.

tion when a mistake is reported.[1] To address this, employees at CCF are encouraged to report events as a method of identifying system issues and/or problems with specific drug classes. Individual performance issues are handled at the unit level. The goal of the system is not to assign blame, but to identify trends. Systems that eliminate the "blame game" have been more successful in getting the employees to report events.[2]

The name of the employee involved in the event is kept confidential, and this information is not published in any reports. Employees understand that any necessary corrective action occurs at the time of the event or the reporting of the event to unit management, not months later when the information is aggregated and analyzed.

Fortunately, researchers agree that the most serious events are reported. Walters,[3] building on the work of Barker and Allan, surveyed nurses on their perceptions of reporting errors and causes of these errors. She found nurses' perceptions and their organizations' definitions of an error were considerably different. Almost all registered nurses would report life-threatening errors or those essential to a patient's treatment, but few would report a daily medication being given late. Informal surveys at CCF revealed that the nursing staff there agree with this view.

Identifying Improvement Opportunities

The purpose of the incident report is to identify opportunities to improve the medication use system. Employees recognize that many changes in the medication distribution system have been instituted because of data included on the incident report. For this reason, the report is not viewed as a punitive action, but as a quality improvement tool. Unit managers receive summary reports of the events. Summary reports are also given to the P&T committee on an annual basis.

The medication events rate is a key measure for determining the success of the medication use system. This is calculated based on patient days [(number of events/patient days) x 100], which is easier to obtain than the doses of medication per unit. It is also a better equalizer when comparing units, eliminating the debate about the percentage of IV medications versus oral medications or the complexity of the drugs involved. Run charts are used to monitor the rate of occurrence and the impact of system changes. Charts are generated for each unit and division level involved. The mean and upper and lower control limits are recalculated annually.

At the nursing unit level, the recalculations use the last two years of data to allow for the reorganization of units or the expansion of services resulting in new staff or management. The upper and lower control limits are only one standard deviation from the mean, which is sensitive to any changes made to the system and shows their impact. When the data points fall within the control limits, the system is in control and staff members have time to decide whether to allocate more resources toward further improvement or to work on other issues. Appropriate actions are taken when special causes are identified. These actions seldom involve major system changes. System changes are based on trends of at least four months of data points outside of the upper control limit, which eliminates knee-jerk reactions that address only the symptoms of the problem and not the root cause. The control chart in Figure 6-2 (page 124) shows the continued lowering of the mean of medication events through the years. Statistical significance is noted when comparing the means between 1992 and 1997 ($t = 2.13$, $df = 3$, $p = .05$). More important to nurses is the clinical significance of decreasing the mean from year to year.

In addition to fear, medication events may go unreported for other reasons as well; many may go unidentified or the nurse may not perceive an event as needing a report. For example, a medica-

Control Chart: Lowering the Mean of Medication Events

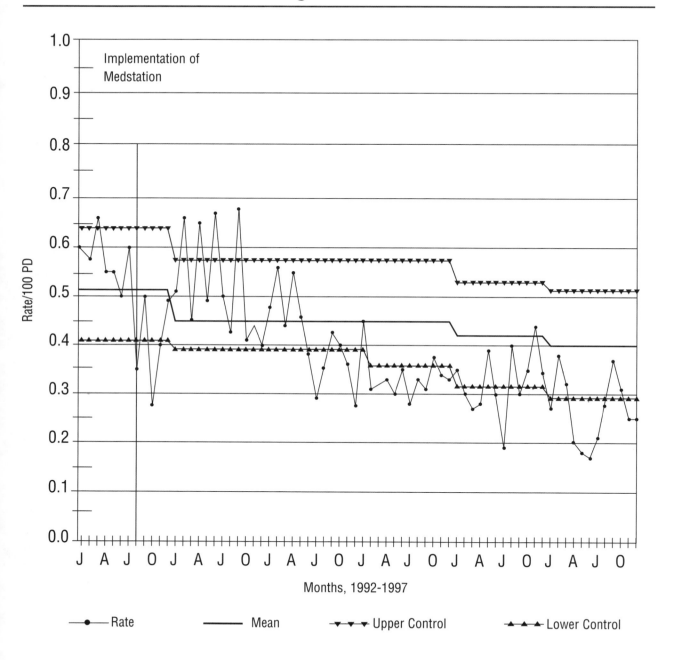

Figure 6-2. *This control chart illustrates a steady decrease in the mean of medication events at The Cleveland Clinic Foundation over a period of several years.*

Source: The Cleveland Clinic Foundation, Ohio.

tion is not given at the appropriate time, or the physician states that a report is not needed.

Monitoring Occurence Rates

The incident reporting system has used the same definitions for the past 12 years, adjusted to correspond with ASHP revisions. When equipment changes are made or new medication protocols are implemented, reports are monitored for an increase in the number of events. For example, after a change in the intravenous tubing for patient-controlled analgesia pumps was made, a number of events were reported indicating the rate was not held, or a free-flow situation had occurred. On examination, it was discovered the new tubing did not have a safety valve to prevent free flow. Within 24 hours, the units were aware of the problem, a temporary extension tubing with the safety valve was put in place, and the vendor was notified. Fortunately, none of these events resulted in adverse patient outcomes, but they did have a high risk level.

Rate of occurrence is monitored on a monthly basis. A detailed annual summary of the type of events, rate of occurrence, and actions taken by nursing or nursing and pharmacy together is submitted to the P&T committee. This report also includes recommendations for actions needed at a higher level of authority in the organization, which are forwarded to the appropriate group for consideration.

Revising policies and procedures has helped to decrease the rate of occurrence for medication events. However, the greatest decreases have occurred when major system changes have been made, such as with the implementation of an automated medstation for controlled substances.

A Pilot Study

The greatest decrease in the organization's rate of medication events occurred when major system changes were made in the storage and control of central nervous system drugs. In the early 1990s,

the P&T committee decided to pilot an automated dispensing system. The objective of this pilot was to determine whether the system decreased the potential for medication events while increasing efficiency and lowering costs. The committee would only support the decision to move to this system if the nursing staff and pharmacy staff thought it would be advantageous.

The idea behind these systems is to provide the nursing staff with easy access to controlled substances and the pharmacy with tighter inventory control. The controlled substances are placed in a separate dispensing machine, requiring an employee's identification number and password for access. Access is granted only to the medication the nurse has indicated, eliminating the possibility of picking up the wrong box.[5] Of course, the success of the system depends on the pharmacy filling the system correctly and the nurse entering the correct medication name.

Planning

The pilot project became the responsibility of the nursing–pharmacy liaison group. The group reviewed the medication events from the previous year, during which 1,040 medication events were reported, with 202 involving the central nervous system drug class. Most of these involved the controlled substances listed in Table 6-1 (page 126). In reviewing the related factors, misreading the drug label accounted for 37% of these events in this drug class (Table 6-2, page 127). The labeling on the boxes and on the injectable cartridges made it very easy to pick up the wrong drug. The boxes containing the prefilled syringes were all labeled in the same print and color, and the prefilled syringes were clear with black lettering. In many cases, the administration of the wrong medication was not identified until the narcotic accountability counts were performed at the end of the shift.

Table 6-1. Top Four Drug Classes in Medication Events

Drug Class	Number of Events	Percentage of Events
Antibiotics	288	28
Central nervous system	202	19
Cardiac	150	14
Fluid and electrolyte	100	10

Source: Incident Reporting Database, The Cleveland Clinic Foundation, Ohio.

Other nurses reported identifying the wrong medication only because of the amount of solution (1 cc versus 2 cc) in the syringe prior to administering it to the patient.

Manufacturers' labeling practices had been a problem over the years,[6] especially in relation to controlled substances. Various changes had been made to correct the situation, but none had long-term effects. Space on the nursing units was limited, and space that could be secured was even rarer. Different configurations of "narcotic cabinets" and drawers were attempted. Signs reminding staff to double-check labels were effective initially, but were soon overlooked.

The nursing–pharmacy liaison group identified the units with the most frequently reported central nervous system medication events. Nursing staff from the orthopedic, thoracic, and hematology units, as well as nursing education, and a representative from the information technology division were added to the group to work on this project. This group was charged with determining whether an automated medication dispensing system for controlled drugs would decrease the number of central nervous system events involving misreading the drug label. They would recommend whether to implement this system, pilot another system, or change nothing with the current system.

The group discussed the current system and the process for administering controlled substances.

The group felt that, in concept, the automated dispensing system could provide a long-term solution to this major issue. The process for developing the pilot began.

Design

The nursing members of the group were not familiar with an automated medication dispensing system, so the vendor provided an on-site demonstration of the equipment. To actually see the system in use, the group traveled to nearby hospitals of equal size where it had been implemented. This was valuable because they were able to see how the system worked and to learn from the nursing staff how to effectively pilot and implement the system. These site visits were also important in helping the group design a new process.

Before the pilot began, locations for the system needed to be identified on each unit and wiring installed to connect it to the pharmacy and to the hospital's admission, discharge, and registration system. The group also had to decide on the medications to be kept in the station. They decided that pharmacy staff would use historical data to determine par levels. Policies and procedures for narcotic accountability, nurse access, and system maintenance had to be developed. Access codes were given to the registered nurses and LPNs on the three units. The float nurses working on the units during the trial received a temporary access code. The group decided the pharmacy would be the

Table 6-2. Factors Related to Top Two Drug Classes in Medication Events

Factor	Antibiotics		Central Nervous System	
Misreading drug label	40	(14%)	75	(37%)
Order transcription	100	(35%)	8	(4%)
Misreading of medication administration record	85	(30%)	68	(34%)
Knowledge deficit	11	(4%)	20	(10%)
Equipment problems	10	(3%)	20	(10%)
Patient identification	5	(2%)	3	(1%)
Pharmacy	7	(2%)	7	(4%)

Source: Incident Reporting Database, The Cleveland Clinic Foundation, Ohio.

keeper of the access codes and passwords. The unit manager would forward names to the pharmacy once a nurse had completed the training sessions.

The pilot was planned for three months on the three nursing units. Three additional units were selected as control units, which were matched by type—two surgical and one medical—and volume of controlled medication use. To evaluate the effectiveness of the system, the rate of events involving controlled medications on the test and control units was measured three months prior to the pilot and the three months during the pilot.

Temporary policies were developed for the accountability of the drugs. These would later serve as templates for organizationwide policies. Nursing and pharmacy staff attended inservices on the system and the changes in the process. At the start of the pilot, the vendor representatives were available to answer any questions from the nursing staff and to troubleshoot.

Implementation

During the first two weeks, two major problems were identified. There were problems with transfer of information between the hospital admission system and the medstation. Until this was solved, the nurses were given dummy patient numbers to obtain medications for new patients. At the same

time, many of the nurses' access codes were rejected. The information services member of the pilot group and the company vendor representative were able to solve this problem. Both of these events were very frustrating to the nursing staff and set the pilot period back two weeks.

The remainder of the trial proceeded without major incident. Many suggestions were made by the nursing staff during the trial period regarding such refinements as drawer configuration, access codes, and medications to stock.

At the end of the trial period, the data from the incident reports were compiled. Due to the small number of events on each unit, the data were collapsed by pilot units and control units to increase the sample size. Table 6-3 (page 128) shows the number of medication events on the three pilot units and the control units. In analyzing the pre- and postpilot data, the monthly rates for the control units decreased. Using a t test, these results were found not to be statistically significant. However, on the test units, the rate decrease was found to be statistically significant ($t = 4.13$, $df = 4$, $p > .05$).

Nursing unit staff were asked whether the system was beneficial and whether it should be implemented across the hospital. The nurses voted unanimously to keep the system. They also offered suggestions for process refinements. The

Table 6-3. Pilot Units

Units	Prepilot		Postpilot	
	No. of Events	Rate of Events	No. of events	Rate of Events
Pilot units	21	0.29/100 PD	6	0.09/100 PD
Control units	18	0.23/100 PD	14	0.18/100PD

Source: Incident Reporting Database, Cleveland Clinic Foundation, Ohio.

pharmacy department also supported the automating of the medication floor stock process because it used resources more effectively while enhancing accountability.

The group recommended implementing the automated medication distribution system over a period of four to five months to give adequate time to set up the system and train all personnel. The recommendation was approved by the P&T committee and negotiations for acquiring the appropriate number of stations began.

The extended implementation period decreased strains on the budget staff, the vendor, and the pharmacy and nursing staff. Real-time inventory levels were a major change from the manual process. No longer was a person required to go to each of the units and determine what controlled substances were needed, return to pharmacy, refill the order, and return to the unit. In the old system, the pharmacy technician had to wait for a nurse to sign off on receiving the controlled drugs. With the automated system refill, information is available immediately without the need to evaluate and prepare an order for restocking.

During implementation, a dual system for narcotic control was needed. Units converted to the automated system ran reports at the end of each shift. Units that had not yet been converted performed manual counts. Both were documented on different forms. This turned out to be more problematic for the pharmacy's record keeping than for the nursing units.

Follow-Up

The implementation of the system has had the desired long-term effect of decreasing the number of events related to misreading of the label. In 1997, central nervous system drug classes were the fifth most frequently reported class, accounting for only 7% of the reported events. Misreading of the label involved 10% of the events.

The organization is now planning to automate other parts of the medication distribution process. This process is more complex due to a more complicated and complex patient population, economic concerns, and quality concerns.

Effective Medication Use Systems

Medication use systems impact all areas of care within an organization—inpatient, outpatient, surgery, emergency department, and so forth. If the system does not have effective checks and balances it can get out of control. As medications become more complex and more difficult to administer and monitor, it is absolutely necessary for all health care professionals involved to communicate their needs, concerns, and suggestions for improvements.

To be effective, a medication use system must have an oversight body that links the medical staff, nursing staff, and pharmacy staff. The P&T

committee fulfills this function by setting the direction of the medication use program. This direction is determined by feedback received from the pharmacy and from the committees involved in quality management and risk management. Changes in the processes involved, from prescribing to monitoring, need to be made continually to keep pace with today's changing health care environment.

One function of the CCF quality improvement program is monitoring the effectiveness of the medications use system. The incident reporting system is the major tool for monitoring risk for the medication use system. When used with other information, such as cost and satisfaction, the quality improvement program can draw a more accurate picture of what is occurring with medication use and where changes need to be made.

References

1. Gaucher EJ, Coffey R: Organizational culture. *Total Quality in Healthcare: From Theory to Practice.* San Francisco: Jossey-Bass Publishers, 1993, p 172.

2. Chandler J: Better than blame. . .Banish a system that blames. *Nursing* 25(5):6, 1996.

3. Walters J: Nurses' perceptions of reportable medication errors and factors that contribute to their occurrence. *Appl Nurs Res* 5(2):86–88, 1992.

4. Lilley L, Guanci R: Watch those labels. *Am J Nurs* 96(5):14, 1996.

5. Lilley L, Guanci R: Med errors. When "look-alikes" and "sound-alikes" don't act alike. *Am J Nurs* 97(*Nurse Practice* extra ed):12, 14, 1997.

6. Rein A, Tiburzi T, Parks V: Comparison of technologies in medication administration. *Nurs Econ* 10(3):233–235, 1992.

GLOSSARY

active failure An error which is precipitated by the commission of errors and violations. These are difficult to anticipate and have an immediate adverse impact on safety by breaching, bypassing, or disabling existing defenses.

adverse drug event (ADE) Any incident in which the use of a medication (drug or biologic) at any dose, a medical device, or a special nutritional product (for example, dietary supplement, infant formula, medical food) may have resulted in an adverse outcome in a patient. *Synonym:* adverse drug error.

adverse drug reaction (ADR) An undesirable response associated with use of a drug that either compromises therapeutic efficacy, enhances toxicity, or both.

adverse event An untoward, undesirable, and usually unanticipated event, such as the death of a patient, an employee, or a visitor in a health care organization. Incidents such as patient falls or improper administration of medications are also considered adverse events even if there is no permanent effect on the patient.

aggregate data Data collected and reported by organizations as a sum or total over a given time period, for example, monthly or quarterly.

benchmarking Continuous measurement of a process, product, or service compared to those of the toughest competitor, to those considered industry leaders, or to similar activities within the organization in order to find and implement ways to improve it. This is one of the foundations of both total quality management and continuous quality improvement. *Internal benchmarking* occurs when similar processes within the same organization are compared. *Competitive benchmarking* occurs when an organization's processes are compared with best practices within the industry. *Functional benchmarking* refers to benchmarking a similar function or process, such as scheduling, in another industry.

causation The act by which an effect is produced. In epidemiology, the doctrine of causation is used to relate certain factors (predisposing, enabling, precipitating, or reinforcing factors) to disease occurrence. The doctrine of causation is also important in the fields of negligence and criminal law. *Synonym:* causality.

clinical pathway A treatment regime, agreed upon by consensus, that includes all the elements of care, regardless of the effect on patient outcomes. It is a broader look at care and may include tests and x-rays that do not affect patient recovery. *Synonym:* clinical path.

complication A detrimental patient condition that arises during the process of providing health care, regardless of the setting in which the care is provided. For instance, perforation, hemorrhage, bacteremia, and adverse reactions to medication (particularly in the elderly) are four complications of colonoscopy and its associated anesthesia and sedation. A complication may prolong an inpatient's length of stay or lead to other undesirable outcomes.

epidemiology Field of medicine concerned with the determination of causes, incidence, and characteristic behavior of disease outbreaks affecting human populations. It includes the interrelationships of host, agent, and environment as related to the distribution and control of disease. *Clinical epidemiology* is a decision-making process applied by an individual practicing physician, where decisions are based on the likelihood of a patient having a given disease process, given a patient's age, previous state of health, family history, the season, the previous appearance of similar diseases in the community, and other factors.

error of commission An error which occurs as a result of an action taken. Examples include when a drug is administered at the wrong time, in the wrong dosage, or using the wrong route; surgeries performed on the wrong side of the body; and transfusion errors involving blood cross-matched for another patient.

error of omission An error which occurs as a result of an action not taken, for example, when a delay in performing an indicated cesarean section results in a fetal death, when a nurse omits a dose of a medication that should be administered, or when a patient suicide is associated with a lapse in carrying out frequent patient checks in a psychiatric unit. Errors of omission may or may not lead to adverse outcomes.

iatrogenic Resulting from the professional activities of physicians, or, more broadly, from the activities of health professionals. Originally applied to disorders induced in the patient by autosuggestion based on a physician's examination, manner, or discussion, the term is currently applied to any undesirable condition in a patient occurring as the result of treatment by a physician (or other health professional), especially to infections acquired by the patient during the course of treatment.

immediate cause *See* proximate cause.

incident report The documentation for any unusual problem, incident, or other situation that is likely to lead to undesirable effects or that varies from established policies and procedures or practices. *Synonym:* occurrence report.

indicator 1. A measure used to determine, over time, performance of functions, processes, and outcomes. **2.** A statistical value that provides an indication of the condition or direction over time of performance of a defined process or achievement of a defined outcome.

latent failure An error which originates in a management and organizational process and poses the greatest danger to complex systems. Latent failures cannot be foreseen but, if detected, they can be corrected before they contribute to mishaps.

local trigger An intrinsic defect or atypical condition that can create failures.

malpractice Improper or unethical conduct or unreasonable lack of skill by a holder of a professional or official position; often applied to physicians, dentists, lawyers, and public officers to denote negligent or unskillful performance of duties when professional skills are obligatory. Malpractice is a cause of action for which damages are allowed.

medication error As defined by the National Coordinating Council for Medication Error Reporting and Prevention (NCC MERP), any preventable event that may cause or lead to inappropriate medication use or patient harm while the medication is in the control of the health care professional, patient, or consumer. Such events may be related to professional practice, health care products, procedures, and systems. These systems may include prescribing; order communication; product labeling, packaging, and nomenclature compounding; dispensing; distribution; administration; education; monitoring; and use.

negligence Failure to use such care as a reasonably prudent and careful person would use under similar circumstances.

observation method An active method of error surveillance in which a trained observer watches the care delivery process.

occurrence screening A system for concurrent or retrospective identification of adverse patient occurrences (APOs) through medical chart-based review according to objective screening criteria. Examples of criteria include admission for adverse results of outpatient management, readmission for complications, incomplete management of problems on previous hospitalization, or unplanned removal, injury, or repair of an organ or structure during surgery. Criteria are used organization-wide or adapted for departmental or topic-specific screening. Occurrence screening identifies about 80% to 85% of APOs. It will miss APOs that are not identifiable from the medical record.

outcome The result of the performance (or non-performance) of a function(s) or process(es).

plan-do-study-act (PDSA) cycle A four-part method for discovering and correcting assignable causes to improve the quality of processes. *Synonyms:* Deming cycle; Shewhart cycle.

potential adverse drug event Serious medication errors which *could* have caused an injury, but did not, by chance or by interception.

process A goal-directed, interrelated series of actions, events, mechanisms, or steps.

proximate cause An act or omission that naturally and directly produces a consequence. It is the superficial or obvious cause for an occurrence. Treating only the "symptoms," or the proximate special cause, may lead to some short-term improvements, but will not prevent the variation from recurring.

retrospective review A method of determining medical necessity or appropriate billing practice for services that have already been rendered.

risk containment Immediate actions taken to safeguard patients from a repetition of an unwanted occurrence. Actions may involve removing and sequestering drug stocks from pharmacy shelves and checking or replacing oxygen supplies or specific medical devices.

risk management Clinical and administrative activities undertaken to identify, evaluate, and reduce the risk of injury to patients, staff, and visitors and the risk of loss to the organization itself.

root cause The most fundamental reason for the failure or inefficiency of a process.

root cause analysis A process for identifying the basic or causal factor(s) that underlie variation in performance, including the occurrence or possible occurrence of a sentinel event.

sentinel event An unexpected occurrence involving death or serious physical or psychological injury, or the risk thereof. Serious injury specifically includes loss of limb or function. The phrase "or the risk thereof" includes any process variation for which a recurrence would carry a significant chance of a serious adverse outcome.

surveillance Ongoing monitoring using methods distinguished by their practicability, uniformity, and rapidity, rather than by complete accuracy. The purpose of surveillance is to detect changes in a trend or distribution to initiate investigative or control measures. *Active surveillance* is systematic and involves review of each case within a defined time frame. *Passive surveillance* is not systematic. Cases may be reported through written incident reports, verbal accounts, electronic transmission, or telephone hotlines, for example.

taxonomy The science of the classification of organisms according to their resemblances and differences, with the application of names or other labels.

underlying cause The systems or process cause that allow for the proximate cause of an event to occur. Underlying causes may involve special-cause variation, common-cause variation, or both.

variation The differences in results obtained in measuring the same phenomenon more than once. The sources of variation in a process over time can be grouped into two major classes: common causes and special causes. Excessive variation frequently leads to waste and loss, such as the occurrence of undesirable patient health outcomes and increased cost of health services. *Common-cause variation,* also called endogenous cause variation or systemic cause variation, in a process is due to the process itself, is produced by interactions of variables of that process, and is inherent in all processes. It is not a disturbance in the process. It can be removed only by making basic changes in the process. *Special-cause variation,* also called exogenous-cause variation or extrasystemic cause variation, in performance results from assignable causes. Special-cause variation is intermittent, unpredictable, and unstable. It is not inherently present in a system; rather, it arises from causes that are not part of the system as designed.

SUGGESTED READINGS

Allan EL, Barker KN: Fundamentals of medication error research. *Am J Hosp Pharm* 47:555–571, 1990.

Altman DG: Strategies for community health intervention: Promises, paradoxes, pitfalls. *Psychosom Med* 57(3):226–33, 1995.

American Society of Health-System Pharmacists: ASHP guidelines on medication-use evaluation. *Am J Health Syst Pharm* 53:1953–1955, 1996.

American Society of Health-System Pharmacists: ASHP guidelines on preventing medication errors in hospitals. *Am J Hosp Pharm* 50:305–314, 1993.

Banks NJ: Methodology matters—IV: Constructing algorithm flowcharts for clinical performance measurement. *I J Qual Health Care* 8(4):395–400, 1996.

Barker KN, Allan EL: Research on drug-use-system errors. *Am J Health Syst Pharm* 52(4):400–403, 1995.

Bates DW, et al: Evaluation of screening criteria for adverse events in medical patients. *Med Care* 33(55):452–462, 1995.

Bates DW, et al: Incidence of adverse drug events and potential adverse drug events. *JAMA* 274(1):29–34, 1995.

Bates DW: Medication errors. How common are they and what can be done to prevent them? *Drug Saf* 5:303–310, 1996.

Bond CA, Raehl CL, Pitterle ME: 1992 National Clinical Pharmacy Services study. *Pharmacotherapy* 14:282–304, 1994.

Bradbury K, et al: Prevention of medication errors: Developing a continuous-quality-improvement approach. *Mt Sinai J Med* 60(5):379–386, 1993.

Cohen MR: Drug product characteristics that foster drug-use-system errors. *Am J Health Syst Pharm* 52(4):395–399, 1995.

Cooper JB, Gaba DM: A strategy for preventing anesthesia accidents. In Lebowitz PW (ed): *International Anesthesiology Clinics.* Boston: Little Brown, 1989, pp 148–152.

Cooper JB, et al: Preventable anesthesia mishaps: A study of human factors. *Anesthesiology* 49(6):399–406, 1978.

Cooper JB, Newbower RS, Ritz RJ: An analysis of major errors and equipment failures in anesthesia management—Considerations for prevention and detection. *Anesthesiology* 60(1):34–42, 1984.

Cooper MC: Can a zero defects philosophy be applied to drug errors? *J Adv Nurs* 21(3):487–491, 1995.

Cullen D, et al: The incident reporting system does not detect adverse drug events: A problem for quality improvement. *Jt Comm J Qual Improv* 21(10):541–548, 1995.

Day G, Hindmarsh J, Hojna C, Roy G, Ventimiglia N: Improving medication administration through an enhanced occurrence reporting system. *J Nurs Care Qual* 9(1):51–56, 1994.

Dew JR: In search of the root cause. *Quality Progress* 24(3): 97–102, 1991.

Galloway D: *Mapping Work Processes.* Milwaukee: ASQC Quality Press, 1997.

Ferner RE: Is there a cure for drug errors? *Br Med J* 311(7003):463–464, 1995.

Fox GN: Minimizing prescribing errors in infants and children. *Am Fam Physician* 53(4):1319–1325, 1996.

Gaba DM: Human error in anesthetic mishaps. In Lebowitz PW (ed): *International Anesthesiology Clinics.* Boston: Little Brown, 1989, pp 137–147.

Gaba DM, DeAnda A: The response of anesthesia trainees to simulated critical incidents. *Anesth Analg* 68(4):444–451, 1989.

Gaucher EJ, Coffey RJ (eds): *Total Quality in Healthcare: From Theory to Practice.* San Francisco: Jossey-Bass, 1993.

GOAL/QPC: *The Memory Jogger.* Methuen, MA: GOAL/QPC, 1988.

Hackel R, Butt L, Banister G: How nurses perceive medication errors. *Nurs Manage* 27(1):31–34, 1996.

Jha AK, Kuperman GJ, Teich JM, et al: Adverse drug events: Development of a computer-based monitor and comparison with chart review and stimulated voluntary report. *J Am Med Inform Assoc* 5:305–314, 1998.

Joint Commission on Accreditation of Healthcare Organizations: *The Measurement Mandate: On the Road to Performance Improvement in Health Care.* Oakbrook Terrace, IL: Joint Commission, 1993.

Joint Commission on Accreditation of Healthcare Organizations: *Sentinel Events: Evaluating Cause and Planning Improvement.* Oakbrook Terrace, IL: Joint Commission, 1998.

Joint Commission on Accreditation of Healthcare Organizations: *Topics in Clinical Care Improvement: Storing and Securing Medications.* Oakbrook Terrace, IL: Joint Commission, 1996.

Joint Commission on Accreditation of Healthcare Organizations: *Using Performance Improvement Tools.* Oakbrook Terrace, IL: Joint Commission, 1996.

Joint Commission on Accreditation of Healthcare Organizations: *Using Quality Improvement Tools in a Health Care Setting.* Oakbrook Terrace, IL: Joint Commission, 1992.

Kelly WN: Pharmacy contributions to adverse medication events. *Am J Health Syst Pharm* 52(4):385–390, 1995.

Klein EG, Santora JA, Pascale PM, Kitrenos JG: Medication cart-filling time, accuracy and cost with an automated dispensing system. *Am J Hosp Pharm* 51:1193–1196, 1994.

Koch KE: Use of standardized screening procedures to identify adverse drug reactions. *Am J Hosp Pharm* 47:1314–1320, 1990.

Lawler N, Newcomb C: *Data Driven Quality Improvement: Flow diagram for using indicator data.* Unpublished, 1994.

Leape LL: Error in medicine. *JAMA* 272(23):1851–1857, 1994.

Leape LL, et al: The nature of adverse events in hospitalized patients: Results of the Harvard

Medical Practice Study. *N Engl J Med* 324(6):377–384, 1991.

Leape LL, et al: Preventing medical injury. *Qual Rev Bull* 19:144–149, 1993.

Leape LL, et al: Systems analysis of adverse drug events. *JAMA* 274(1):35–43, 1995.

Lilley L, Guanci R: Med errors. When "look-alikes" and "sound-alikes" don't act alike. *Am J Nurs* 97(*Nurse Practice* extra ed):12, 14, 1997.

Marek CL: Avoiding prescribing errors: A systematic approach. *JADA* 127(5):617–623, 1996.

Nelson EC, Batalden PB, Ryer JC (eds): *Clinical Improvement Action Guide.* Oakbrook Terrace, IL: Joint Commission on Accreditation of Healthcare Organizations, 1998.

Pepper GA: Errors in drug administration by nurses. *Am J Health Syst Pharm* 52(4):390–395, 1995.

Reason J: *Human Error.* Cambridge, MA: Cambridge University Press, 1992.

Reason J: Human and organizational factors: Lessons from other domains. Presented at the Examining Errors in Health Care Conference, Rancho Mirage, CA: Oct 13–15, 1996.

Reichheld FF: Learning from customer defections. *Harv Bus Rev* 74(2):56–69, 1996.

Riegelman RK: *Minimizing Medical Mistakes: The Art of Medical Decision Making.* Boston: Little, Brown and Company, 1991.

Roland C, Cronin K, Guberman C, et al: Insights into improving organizational performance. *Quality Prog* 30(3):82–85, 1997.

Roseman C, Booker JM: Workload and environmental factors in hospital medication errors. *Nurs Res* 44(4):1226–1230, 1995.

Rupp RO, Russell JR: The golden rules of process redesign. *Qual Prog* 27(12):85–90, 1994.

Schneider PJ, Hartwig SC: Use of severity indexed medication error reports to improve quality. *Hosp Pharm* 29:205–215, 1994.

Schwid HA, O'Donnell D: Anesthesiologists' management of simulated critical incidents. *Anesthesiology* 76(4):495–501, 1992.

Sellers G: Using flowcharts for performance improvement. *Quality Digest* 17(3):49–51, 1997.

Senders JW: Detecting, correcting, and interrupting errors. *J Intraven Nurs* 18(1):28–32, 1995.

Sittig DF, Stead WW: Computer-based physician order entry: The state of the art. *J Am Med Inform Assoc* 1:108–123, 1994.

Trick OL: Adverse drug reactions: Establishing a hierarchy of definitions for adjustment of report rates. *Hosp Pharm* 31(12):1593–1595, 1996.

Walters J: Nurses' perceptions of reportable medication errors and factors that contribute to their occurrence. *Appl Nurs Res* 5(2):86–88, 1992.

Welsh F: Charting new territory. *Quality Prog* (30)2:63–66, 1997.

Wilson PF, et al: *Root Cause Analysis.* Milwaukee: ASQC Quality Press, 1993.

INDEX

V

W

BUSINESS REPLY MAIL

FIRST CLASS MAIL   PERMIT NO 632   VILLA PARK IL

POSTAGE WILL BE PAID BY ADDRESSEE

ATTN HELEN FRY
JOINT COMMISSION ON ACCREDITATION
OF HEALTHCARE ORGANIZATIONS
ONE RENAISSANCE BOULEVARD
OAKBROOK TERRACE IL 60181–9887

How Well Does *Medication Use: A Systems Approach to Reducing Errors* Meet Your Needs?

We'd like to know what you think of *Medication Use: A Systems Approach to Reducing Errors*. Your comments will help us evaluate and improve the value of this publication. Please take a few minutes to give us your opinion and mail this postage-paid card.

Please indicate whether you agree or disagree with the following statements:

Medication Use	Strongly Agree	Somewhat Agree	Agree	Somewhat Disagree	Strongly Disagree
• provides useful and timely information	☐	☐	☐	☐	☐
• presents new concepts and practical strategies for reducing medication errors	☐	☐	☐	☐	☐
• is a value for its price	☐	☐	☐	☐	☐
• is worth recommending to a colleague	☐	☐	☐	☐	☐

Please rate the value of the following elements:

	Extremely Valuable	Very Valuable	Somewhat Valuable	Not Very Valuable	Not at all Valuable
• Foreword	☐	☐	☐	☐	☐
• Introduction	☐	☐	☐	☐	☐
• Overview of medication use system	☐	☐	☐	☐	☐
• Measuring and monitoring performance	☐	☐	☐	☐	☐
• Defining medication errors	☐	☐	☐	☐	☐
• Preventing medication errors	☐	☐	☐	☐	☐
• Workbook section	☐	☐	☐	☐	☐
• Case study	☐	☐	☐	☐	☐

• Other (please be specific) _____

I use *Medication Use* to (please check all that apply):

☐ Establish a medication use system   ☐ Prevent medication errors
☐ Improve a medication use system   ☐ Educate staff
☐ Measure and monitor a medication   ☐ Other (please be specific)_____
    use system

My job title: _____

Type and size of organization: _____

State(s) in which we operate: _____

Please make any additional comments about *Medication Use*.

_____
_____
_____

If we may contact you for additional feedback about this or any other Joint Commission publication or for suggestions for future publications, please provide the following information:

Name: _____
Organization: _____
Address: _____
_____ Telephone number: _____

If you would like more information about Joint Commission publications, please call our Customer Service Center at 630/792-5800.

Thank you!